FALLING IN AGAIN
tales of an incorrigible angler

Also published by **Merlin Unwin Books**
7 Corve Street, Ludlow, Shropshire SY8 1DB.
Telephone orders: 01584 877456 or you can order via our website:
www.countrybooksdirect.com

The Secret Carp
Chris Yates
ISBN 1873674287 £17.99

An Angler for all Seasons
the best of H. T. Sheringham
H. T. Sheringham
ISBN 187367404X £16.95

The One That Got Away
or tales of days when fish triumphed over anglers
Brian Clarke, Jeremy Paxman, Max Hastings, David Steel, et al
ISBN 1873674023 £16.95

A History of Flyfishing
Conrad Voss Bark
ISBN 1873674031 £16.00 hardback £12.95 paperback

The Pocket Guide to Fishing Knots
Peter Owen   ISBN 1873674341 £5.99

Hook, Line and Thinker: Angling & Ethics
Alexander Schwab
ISBN 1873674597 £17.99

Dear Jim, Reflections on the Beauty of Angling
Alexander Schwab
ISBN 1873674791 £20.00

FALLING IN AGAIN
tales of an incorrigible angler

Written & Illustrated by

Chris Yates

MERLIN UNWIN BOOKS

First published in Great Britain by Merlin Unwin Books (1998)
ISBN 1873674333
Reprinted 2002, 2004

Published by:
Merlin Unwin Books
Palmers House, 7 Corve Street
Ludlow, Shropshire SY8 1DB (U.K.)
www.countrybooksdirect.com
email: books@merlinunwin.co.uk

British Library Cataloguing-in-Publication Data:
A catalogue record for this book is available from the British
Library

ISBN 1873674333

Designed and typeset by Merlin Unwin Books, Ludlow
Printed in Great Britain by Cromwell Press, Trowbridge

Contents

Acknowledgements

I would like to thank all my loyal, unselfish, mad angling friends who, as revealed in the following pages, have provided me with moral support, landing nets, pots of tea and other items essential to the survival of one so ill-equipped.

I am also indebted to the editors of various angling magazines who, for dubious reasons, encouraged me to write some of the stories published here. I would particularly like to thank Jon Ward Allen of *Waterlog*, Colin Mitchell of *Coarse Angling*, Kevin Wilmot of *Improve Your Coarse Fishing* and David Hall of *David Hall's Coarse Fishing*.

I would also like to thank my two uncannily perceptive typists, Pat Taylor and Tina Mulliner, who somehow deciphered my scrawled manuscripts. (Would a word processor help? Not under a leaky umbrella or up a tree!)

And finally I take my fishing hat off to the patience and forbearance of my publisher and editor Merlin Unwin.

> DEDICATION
> ───────────
> To my mother

We shall not cease from exploration
And the end of all our exploring
Will be to arrive where we started
And know the place for the first time.

Little Gidding T. S. Eliot

Introduction

One of angling's great attractions is the fact that no two fishing days are exactly alike; there will always be some new challenge, marvel or mystery, no matter how similar the initial prospects. At the same time there are the changeless, enduring and constant pleasures that are made even more precious by our impermanent world.

And then there is the angler himself, with his own particular joys, obsessions and eccentricities. His style of fishing may change, he may transfer his devotion from one species to another, but he will always be an angler. Season after season he just wants to repeat the happy uncomplicated exercise of catching - or at least trying to catch - a fish.

I have been an angler for forty years and my enthusiasm is as strong now as it was when I made my first cast. However, at this stage in my watery life I would say I am more experimental, more confident, perhaps even a little more proficient. Looking back, I see there are many lessons I never learnt, or never remembered. I continue to make the same kind of mistakes at crucial moments, I continue to have too much faith in old methods, I am still a sucker for monster stories, I still put too much trust in untrustworthy fish. I can also suffer the same kind of doubts, uncertainties and feelings of inadequacy that I first knew when I was a fisher-boy. Similarly, my elation, not only at catching a good fish but sometimes just at the prospect of going fishing, remains childishly intense. I am also heartened by the recurrence of odd little events which prove the effectiveness of my angler's instinct, and intrigued by repeated occurrences that point to a possible relationship between my instinct and that of the fish.

The quirky habits of wild freshwater fish always fascinate me, and so do the repeated instances of inexplicable angling coincidences.

All these things reveal subtle patterns throughout my fishing, mysteriously circular patterns that are taking me forwards, and back to where I began. I don't claim anything unique in this. I think the same kind of patterns are woven into every angler's life. My theme, therefore, is familiar, no matter how personal the following stories might be. The only real uniqueness here is in the way I so often fail to learn from my mistakes. For instance, I fell in again last Thursday.

Chris Yates
September 1998

CHAPTER 1

The Coach Trip

For years I had been dissolving in water. Mesmerised by local ponds and rivers, haunted by the occasionally glimpsed marvels of the deep, I was wasting away, becoming more and more convinced I would never make a proper angler. There had, it was true, been gudgeon, minnows and even perch, but nothing to show I had truly unlocked the water's secrets. Furthermore, I had no family or friends who could advise me. There had been an angling neighbour and though he had helped me catch my first fish he had now disappeared. But then I discovered a new ally.

Fred Jones was our local electrician. One day in my eleventh summer, he came over to our house to unravel some mysterious business concerning popping light bulbs and smoking sockets. During the obligatory tea break he talked about things other than blown fuses and, in the course of the conversation, we discovered that Fred was not only an angler but the secretary of the Banstead Angling Society. He described the organisation as a friendly bunch who met every fortnight to journey by coach to a variety of other worlds. Fred showed me the new season's fixture list containing such exotic and evocative sounding names as The Pevensy Haven, Barcombe Mills, Whyke Pit, Swan Meadows. I had never heard of any of these places before, but they conjured up wonderful images of dark, smooth, monster-haunted waters. By the time he left our house I had become a new junior member. Fred was pleased to sign me up and my mother was happy enough about the idea to pay my subscription which entitled me to a certificate, a club rule book and another headful of extravagant dreams.

On the first Sunday of the season I rose early, gathered my rod, tackle, sandwiches and bottle of ginger beer and set off to meet the coach. At the appointed place (outside Fred's house) a group of men were already waiting. Each one stood by a vast and substantial creel, each had a colossal rod holdall slung over his shoulder - holdalls that probably contained the entire stock of the Alcock's catalogue. There were also green canvas buckets full of stodgy groundbait and a few neatly bound heaps consisting of stormcoats and waders.

Now I was accustomed to seeing real fishermen at the local pond, anglers who possessed expensive looking rods, landing nets, boxfuls of floats and metal rod rests, but these giants of the Banstead Angling Society were so extravagantly equipped I felt ashamed to stand next to them. With my old 8ft spinning rod and all my bits in a school satchel, I was seriously unprepared, like a boy with a pop gun joining the army.

The anglers bade me a cheery good morning and all seemed pleased about life in general, but I guessed they were enjoying a quiet joke at my expense. Fred Jones appeared on the scene, also carrying a mountain of gear. As if this was a sign, everyone looked first at their watches and then expectantly along the street. The coach chugged into view and there was a creaking of wicker as everyone heaved their creels onto their shoulders. We loaded up and piled in and were away through the deserted roads of dawn, bound for the River Medway in Kent.

The coach had already been half full and I hoped there might be some other junior member on board for whom this was also his first trip. I was bewildered by the mysterious discussions concerning 'the sweep'. I was troubled about the questions of river board licences, the amount of maggots I'd need to buy (bait was sold on the coach), the techniques used to catch Medway roach. It would have been comforting to have shared my ignorance with someone equally naïve. But all the other juniors were obviously well versed in club lore. They looked confident and blasé. Some of them smoked quite openly and made debunking jokes about the committee - that important group of elders in earnest debate at the front of the coach. So I made my decisions without consultation.

Though not understanding what 'the sweep' was all about, I agreed to take part, at the cost of an extra shilling. I admitted to not having a Kent River Board

Licence and was sold one for two shillings. I bought sixpence worth of maggots and was advised also to purchase a book of size 12 hooks to nylon as these 'were best for your average Medway roach'. Though I wouldn't have a penny left, I paid willingly, being eager to get amongst them. However, I didn't admit that I'd never even seen a roach before.

I'd never seen the Medway before, either, and the journey to the middle reaches, at Barming, took me through the unfamiliar Kent landscape, with its orchards, hop fields and oast houses. It seemed we'd travelled hundreds of miles by the time we got there. By then the atmosphere in the coach was so thick with tobacco smoke I could hardly breathe. I stumbled out, filling my lungs with life-sustaining air, convinced that the Medway was the sweetest smelling river in England. And what a river! It was five times as wide as the Mole, which was the only other river I'd fished, and looked even more exciting. It was deep, the banks shaded by tall trees and bordered by reed and lily beds. I hung over the bridge next to the coach and stared down at the water, imagining shoals of monster roach.

We'd picked a number from a bag during the trip and now we were 'called off' according to our number, with about ten seconds between us. Gradually the crowd of heavily laden anglers diminished. Then my number was called and I joined the long, staggered column of fishermen, all trudging across the bridge and down the riverbank.

Naturally I had no idea where I was going. I passed

'Number One', who was briskly setting up his gear in a swim where a jutting bank formed a quiet eddy. Already he had a triumphant gleam in his eyes. 'Number Two' was a few swims further on and he, too, looked as if he was assured a momentous catch. The first dozen men away all looked immensely pleased with life as they settled in their chosen swims, but there were a few less happy expressions amongst the later arrivals.

My choice of swim was dictated by its proximity to Fred. He would probably give me a few tips about roach fishing and maybe lend a hand when I fell in. Luckily there was no one in the swim below him, so I plonked myself down and prepared to fish.

The sight of the river and the bright summer morning had made me forget my earlier feelings of inadequacy. Suddenly I was optimistic. Maybe I would catch an enormous roach, win the sweepstake and be carried back to the coach shoulder high.

I asked Fred how you fished for Medway roach. 'Like you fish for them anywhere else,' he said. 'Fine and light.'

Right then, five-pound line was all I had on my reel, but I'd got those 12 hooks tied to finer nylon and one of my four floats was a crow quill. I baited with two maggots and cast out. My float drifted down into the lilies and I instantly lost the hook in the stems. Next cast I had a tremendous bite and missed it. Then I had another, less noticeable bite. In fact I didn't notice anything at all, but when I lifted the tackle out at the end of the swim, there was a small silver fish on the line.

'Look, Fred!' I shouted joyfully. 'I've caught a roach already.'

'No you haven't,' he said, sympathetically. 'That's a bleak.'

Roach, bleak, what did I care? They were all new and wonderful things to me and it didn't matter that I went on catching bleak all morning. And even though Fred said that bleak didn't count in the sweep I still felt quite proud of myself, especially as he hadn't caught anything yet.

I put my rod down and ate my sandwiches, feeling like a seasoned society angler. A courting couple in a boat came drifting down the middle of the river, a transistor radio shattering the calm. Fred was just rising from his creel, intending to impolitely demand silence, when a sudden and powerful gust of wind, a miniature whirlwind, swept over the water and struck the boat amidships. Though the couple were not indecently undressed they had shed a fair amount of clothing and now all of it simply spiralled up into the skies along with a Sunday paper. The girl shrieked, the bloke yelled. I lay back on the bank watching with interest as all the clothes and pages gently descended into the river. Fate must smile like this on all society outings, I thought, as I happily drained my ginger beer.

The bleak went off the feed in the scorching afternoon and I didn't get any more bites. Fred caught an eel, which I thought an astonishing achievement, although he seemed to think otherwise. News came down the bank that 'Malcolm was really knocking them out'. He, I discovered,

6

was the man first away in the morning.

As the afternoon progressed I began to get restless and impatient. I also began to develop a raging thirst and regretted downing my ginger beer in one gulp. Fred, however, began to fish more earnestly as if he knew he could catch fish if he concentrated harder. He followed his float downstream with the tip of a colossal roach rod. The whole Tonkin butt looked as substantial as a scaffold pole and the tip seemed to stretch halfway across the river. (He must have had arms like Superman.) He was probably only trying to appear serious, though, hoping that if he did so I might take the hint and stop pestering him with questions. He possibly wished that he'd never even mentioned fishing to me in the first place. But then his float disappeared and he upped his rod nicely. The tip curved and jagged and in came a magnificent roach.

'What a fish!' I said. The blue sheen on the scales and the rose red fins were simply beautiful. I gazed at it from a distance of about three inches, thinking that though it lacked the magical quality of a carp, I would still have gladly swopped all my Dinky toys for one like it.

Fred whipped out his anglers' ruler and laid the superb specimen along it. 'Not even a goer!' he said, flipping it back in the river. Suddenly a great shoal of roach went mad in Fred's swim and he hauled them out one after the other but not one of them made the coveted eight inch mark, not even if you stretched their tails. I wouldn't have minded whether any roach of mine was a 'goer' or not, but there were to be no roach for me that day, big or small. I was still not a proper angler; yet, with so many proper anglers around me, that status now seemed less impossible.

'That's it,' said Fred, abruptly. 'Six o'clock, time to pack up.' We put away our gear and began to walk back towards the bridge, overtaking several more fortunate anglers along the way. These men were laden not just with creels and holdalls but were also carrying their groundbait buckets now full of water and alive with 'goers'. I glimpsed the dark shapes of the roach within. Some were circling round and round, one or two were too tremendous to move at all, just purple crescents lodged against the canvas sides.

By the bridge two committee members were assembling a complex structure of bars, chains and weights. It was supported by a tripod and a large wire basket hung from its centre. One by one the anglers weighed their catches and I stared agape at the spectacle. Suddenly Fred's roach seemed almost insignificant; there were fish there over a pound!

Malcolm was waiting till the end, holding his fish in a cavernous keepnet by the bridge. He appeared eventually, to a cheer from the gallery, his expression a nice mix of modesty and victory, his net bulging with miraculous roach. Naturally he won the sweep, collecting the fabulous sum of almost £3.

The fish were released (not looking as pristine as they should, thanks to the wire basket) and we loaded our gear onto the coach. But we didn't set off home straight away. There was a riverside pub nearby and the entire membership poured through the door as purposefully as the Medway flowed through the bridge. As I said, I'd spent all my money on the coach, so although my throat was parched dry, I could do nothing more than hang about outside, dehydrating.

Through the pub's open window I watched the ranks of red faced anglers lifting their jugs to their lips and swallowing the cool looking liquid, but after an interval I had to look away. Fred eventually appeared through the door, a long glass in his hand. Ice chinked against the sides as he came towards me. 'One day you'll catch a roach, son,' he said. 'In the meantime, have some lemonade.'

It was as good as if I'd won the sweep.

CHAPTER 2

The Bass Trip

It was something to do with the tides. Apparently they were the highest – or lowest – of the year and, according to Parker, this meant more bass. 'What about ordinary tides,' I'd said, 'at normal times of the day?'

I'd been disturbed by Parker's insistence that to take advantage of the tide we'd have to be out on the rocks before sunrise which would entail a very early start. I have never been good at early starts, especially on Sundays. But my feeble protests were simply ignored.

'If you're going bass fishing on the Dragon's Teeth,' said Parker, 'you should go when conditions are as near perfect as possible.' He came round to collect me at three o'clock the next morning and we set off in the dark towards Beachy Head.

I should add that I have occasionally caught bass before. I wasn't a complete novice. But I had never caught them properly: in the other words, they had always happened accidentally when I was, say, casting a spinner from a beach for mackerel. I had never set out to fish for them on purpose, nor had I thought that close reading of tide tables could lead me to the best chance of catching one. Parker, however, was purposeful in bass fishing. He knew everything, from the best casting times to the best rigs, from the best baits to the best marks, which included, of course, the one we were heading for. Yet if he seemed a class bassist next to me, he was, next to his brother, Berol, still only dabbling in the basics. Berol, who would be waiting for us on a cliff path later, was serious about every-thing – money, women, football, work and fishing. I remember once at a weedy overgrown farm pond, where there was always a good chance of a carp, he tut-tutted at my floppy rod and cranky reel and said, 'You can't muck about here.'

Mucking about was what I always did, though. It's what I still do. If I have a better understanding of weedy ponds and lowland rivers than I do of rocky shorelines and

mountains streams, it's because of long and happy famil-
iarity rather than deliberations and study. As long as I've
got a line in I'm content and my methods have always been
as simple and straightforward as possible. I don't in fact
like to be conscious of my tackle at all, using it only as an
extension of my feeling for the water. And if I haven't got
any particular feelings then things are not difficult, just
slow, and I simply have to muck about a bit more, with my
line doing the feeling for me, until I begin to get the
picture. But the problem with shore fishing is that you
don't get much time to muck about before the tide comes
in and washes you away.

The sea looked pale and indistinct as we stared out
at it rom the clifftop, with Berol, at sunrise. Down below were
the Dragon's Teeth, of bass fishing legend – jagged fangs of
rock extending out from the chalk cliffsides. They looked
black in contrast to the sea, which, directly below us, was
made milky by the constant erosion of the chalk.

I'd not remembered just how rocky the shoreline
was below Beachy Head, but that, as Parker explained, was
only so evident now because of the extreme tide, with the
lunar influence at its most powerful and therefore the rocks
not only more visible but also more accessible. The whole
point of the day's exercise was therefore made much clearer
to me. We could get right out onto the Teeth, collect soft-
back crabs for bait and begin fishing as the tide began to
turn.

13

We clambered down the steep path, out of the slightly chilly north-westerly breeze, hearing the sound of waves growing steadily louder as we descended, smelling the salty cabbageness from the acres of exposed seaweed.

With the rest of our gear left on a rock, Berol took just a bucket and a cunningly bent length of wire over to the rock pools and for an hour we helped him tweak crabs out from their various craggy boltholes. Hard shelled crabs were no good for bait, said Berol; what the bass liked best were the poor soft backs who were between carapaces, having shed one but not yet formed the next. When we'd laboriously collected a couple of dozen – the crab population had obviously been taking a battering recently – Berol said that, despite the bait shortage, we'd better tackle up. Already the tide had turned and the bass would be advancing.

As I said, I'd never deliberately set myself up for bass so now I had to watch carefully as Parker and Berol made up complex swivel encrusted paternosters weighted down with devilish four-ounce grip leads. Naturally I had no swivels or grip leads, but Berol was impressed with my alternative. In fact he could hardly stop himself laughing at the sight of the one-ounce bored bullet (as a running leger) which I thought would be perfectly adequate. Yet if he was amused by my choice of tackle, he was amazed by my choice of rod.

'What's this?!' he spluttered. 'Is it a carbon rod I

14

see before me? Where's the split cane?' I explained that I wasn't going to risk chaffing one of my lovely bits of bamboo on a barnacled rock, especially when Hardy's had so recently presented me with this eleven-foot carbon whopper stopper. They had hoped I might find it useful for big carp, but it was really much too stiff and unresponsive for my kind of carp fishing. Once Berol had got over the shock of seeing me caneless, he said it would probably do. Naturally, both he and Parker had beefy carbon sea rods, complete with large multiplying reels, while my reel was an old Mitchell 300 loaded with 12lb braided line.

Berol was less critical of the reel than the line which he said, in these circumstances, was a dubious choice, though he didn't explain why.

We got down close to where the waves were breaking over the rocks, baited our hooks and cast out. Parker and Berol cast much further than me, not only because they were using four-ounce leads, big rods and multipliers, but also because they were wearing waders. They had sloshed out to a casting position on a big rock that I couldn't reach in my wellies. Yet when my bait landed in a deep gully between two of the Teeth, I felt reasonably confident – especially when, after only ten minutes, the rod tip was dunked twice and hauled decisively over.

'A fish!' I yelled. Thirty yards out, where the rocks were gnashing the sea into foam, something was pulling slowly and heavily. Both Parker and Berol turned to stare.

They looked appreciatively at the bent and pulsing rod and Parker was about to shout something when the line snapped down at the hook.

I don't think I've ever hooked such a big fish in the sea before. Once I landed a 5lb wrasse off the Cornish coast, but that bass – if it was a bass – felt much larger. Parker and Berol turned back to their fishing without saying anything and I went off for a minute on my own to bite chunks out of the cliff.

The tide, the big spring tide, was coming in quite quickly. I was tackled up and fishing again, on my rock, but after half an hour the two bass pros were about to be marooned, though they seemed oblivious of the fact. They were clearly far too engrossed to notice anything other than their rods, their anticipation no doubt heightened by my dramatic first cast. But what had been a quiet shallow gulley behind their boulder was now a surf filled, deepening torrent, though I waited until just before danger level before shouting a warning. Even then, Parker just peered idly down as if he was on a boat, while Berol simply made a gesture of indifference, reeled in and recast. I suppose my warning could have been more persuasive, so, waiting for only another few inches of tidewater, I shouted again, making reference this time to swimming, drowning and lifeboats. Even then, with the waves beginning to break over them, they seemed reluctant to withdraw. They gathered their things and began to work their way back, and the first

16

wave to catch them went over their waders. I stood happily on my island, watching with interest as Berol stumbled and went down. It was probably the grip leads, I thought. He made it without bubbling, however, and pausing only to drain his waders, he was soon reaching for the bass again. My rock, or rather my ledge, was obviously the place to be. Not only was it still dry, you also hooked bass from it, even landing them if you had the proper gear. Parker caught a brace of about four pounds each – lovely, bristling, golden fish – and Berol caught another of about the same size. I caught a rockling of nearly a pound and as I'd never even seen a rockling before I said it was as good as any bass, though no one else thought so.

The weather had changed since dawn; it had become quite warm, almost muggy and the sun was breaking out. Almost catching us all out, the tide came past my ledge and we had to retreat again. It came on and on until it even passed lunchtime and we realised how hungry we were and how much we desired a cool glass of beer.

Certainly, it had been exciting fishing, with the waves crashing around us, the great cliff rising above us and the thought of the bass cruising unseen through the depths below us. I had even, despite my mistakes, begun to get a feeling of what the sea, with its sudden surges and rock deflected currents, was doing and how it might be affecting the fish, though I still couldn't understand how my line had broken so easily. I would, of course, come again. Before the tide had reached its highest point, however, we were hurrying over the cliffs towards Eastbourne, not because we were in danger of being cut off, but because it was almost closing time.

CHAPTER 3

Happy New Year

My fishing pal, Dick Smith, and half a dozen proper grown-up anglers who should have known better, stood huddled on the street corner waiting for the club coach. It was a freezing cold January morning and as I walked towards the little group of hunched up figures, my rod bag and basket over my shoulder, I thought we must all be mad. The only other sign of life was a half frozen paper boy delivering the Sundays; everyone else, even the cats and dogs, were snug in bed and if they were sensible they would stay in bed all day.

It was one of those bitter winter days that sorts out the men from the boys; a mean, head-pincering wind blew from the east, the light was hard and brittle, the temperature had lost sight of zero. So, being a boy anyway, I was perfectly justified in expressing my trepidation. As I came among the other anglers I went into an exaggerated shudder, shaking my head and legs as if they were on fire and rattling my teeth. Only Dick laughed. The grown ups looked at me as if I was the only nutcase present.

'A Nippy New Year to you,' said Dick.

'Get anything good for Christmas?' I asked, trotting on the spot to keep warm.

'My Mum gave me a weird book about how to fish for black bass and pumpkin seed,' he replied.

'Maybe she's going to take you on holiday to America,' I said.

'Anywhere would be better than Banstead in January,' said Dick, 'even if they do only have fish called pumpkin seed.'

We were interrupted by the arrival of the coach and the next moment we were sitting in a warm, cheery, smoke filled atmosphere, trundling south towards the Sussex Ouse at Isfield.

Banstead Angling Society had been invited to fish the Isfield Angling Society water for a friendly, roving inter-club match. An invitation like that usually meant that the visiting club watched the host club catch a miraculous draught of fishes from their favourite (prebaited?) swims, while the newcomers made do with minnows. But the talk on the journey was of big roach, dace and chub and Fred Jones, the secretary, reminisced on previous visits to the Ouse when all of Banstead had bent their rods.

Ah, I thought, but that was in summer, when you could actually see the shoals of big dace playing on the shallows and when you could put down your rod whenever you liked, because your hand wasn't frozen to it.

The coach eventually pulled up at the end of a muddy farm track not far from the river. Through the windows I could actually feel a warmth from the low sun and the green-grey landscape looked almost welcoming. But when we filed untidily out into the morning I knew my optimism was unfounded. Though the wind wasn't strong, the air was like coarse sandpaper; it made my eyes water even more than the tobacco-rich interior of the coach. And all the puddles along the lane were solid ice.

Cold weather, I thought, trying to recall all that Richard Walker and Bernard Venables and Fred J. Taylor had written about it. I have to find a nice deep slack – but not a completely dead slack. Somewhere just off a bit of current. Blow that! All I need to find is somewhere out of the wind, completely sheltered and in the sun.

'I got this chair as well,' said Dick suddenly, as we trudged along the river bank to where the Isfield AS members were waiting for us.

'Eh?' I said.

'For Christmas,' he added. 'Folds up into my bag as neat as a pancake.'

'As neat as a pancake? Don't you mean as flat?'

'My mum's pancakes are neat,' he said.

'I suppose she uses a special pancake mould!' I said.

'It's still a good chair.'

'Here you are lads,' said a jovial-looking Isfielder

21

holding out a bagful of numbered discs. 'Pick a number, any number, it might be your lucky New Year!'

Dick picked 9, I picked 31. But he didn't walk off when Fred called his number; he waited, like a true friend, for me.

'I want you to see how comfortable I'm going to be in my new chair,' he said.

We walked up-stream, following the river as it twisted through clumps of sheltering alder and curved across bleak, open fields. A man called Eric sounded excited as he told us he'd just seen a sea trout jumping, but all the others we passed just looked rather earnest and serious as they tackled up. They also looked very cold. We eventually discovered a likely-looking glide between high banks of bramble and blackthorn, where we could get down out of the wind and see how long we could make our Thermos flasks last.

Dick's new chair was one of those fishing chairs that mums always buy. Like that fishing book he'd been given, it was a joke. Yet I suppose it was quite comfortable once you'd found yourself a bit of concrete to put it on. Its legs were thin metal strips that sunk slowly into the bank as far as the canvas seat, even though the bank was frozen solid. But worse than this, you needed to be a mechanic to assemble it. There were so many screws and wing nuts to adjust and tighten – all by hand. By the time it was ready our already numb fingers were burning with cold. It would have been tactless to have said: 'Give me my old basket any day,' so I just said: 'Your mum must really love you,' and cackled with laughter.

The Ouse had that black, sullen expression that all rivers probably adopt just before a new Ice Age. We could imagine those miserable cold-blooded fish, lying comatose on the bottom and we began to imagine how much colder we'd feel if we were down there with them. How did those dace and roach and chub manage to exist?

Even with a snorkel, we wouldn't last five seconds down there on a day like this, and we were meant to be warm blooded. The talk degenerated, or, rather, snowballed towards worst-case scenarios of death by freezing, torture by freezing, having to assemble a Meccano tractor in a blizzard wearing only your underpants.

After a couple of hours we suddenly realised we might not be joking. Even though we were both wearing about three pairs of socks, two pairs of jeans, two pullovers and ex-army parkas ('as worn by Swedish commandos'), it was noticeable how still we'd become.

I remembered reading how you slow down and become inert during the first phases of hypothermia and suggested we pack up four hours early.

'Do you think the coach will still be there?' asked Dick as he painfully raised himself from his chair.

'I dunno,' I answered. 'It wouldn't go back to the coach station. That's forty miles. But maybe the coachie's gone off to spend the day in some nice warm café.'

Dick's face, as he struggled to disassemble his neat-as-a-pancake chair, was like cracked ice on a frozen pond. I would have tried to help, but I couldn't actually force my fingers and thumbs to close. Eventually he just pushed his arm between the canvas and the frame and dangled the chair clumsily over his shoulder. I couldn't even break down my rod. Holding our stuff awkwardly under our arms, we began to walk like two robots downriver.

No one else seemed to move as we passed behind them and we presumed, quite naturally, that they'd all frozen to death. But Eric was moving. In fact he turned, red faced and cheery, to greet us.

'Changing swims, lads?' he asked. 'I won't be moving. That sea trout I thought I saw was a great big roach. I've caught four. Reckon I've won the match for Banstead. Have a look!'

In his net were four roach bigger than any roach we'd ever seen before.

'Yeah, Eric,' we said. 'Great! See you at the weigh-in.' And we shuffled off without a second glance.

'Look!' I gasped as we finally reached the farm track. 'The coach!'

'Probably just a mirage,' said Dick, as we hobbled forwards on numb feet.

But it was real, and the coachie opened the door for us after we let our gear fall from our arms and left it lying in the track.

'Happy New Year!' he said. We could hardly believe it. In the middle of the aisle was a large paraffin stove and round it were huddled several other deserters, holding their poor hands to the rising heat.

'Make way for two more lost souls,' said the

24

coachie. 'And pour a couple of mugs of tea, Malcolm.'

Malcolm appeared from behind a Sunday paper and poured tea from a vast brown china teapot. The coachie must have been some sort of saint. The Patron Saint of the Frozen Angler. As Malcolm passed us our steaming mugs he opened a small flask of brandy and added a nip or two to our tea.

'You may be under age,' he said, 'but it's New Year and, anyway, I don't want you both dying on us.'

Gradually, life returned painfully to our limbs. We began to feel normal again. We began to move our toes. We were curious to know whether Eric was going to win the match but we didn't venture outside, not even to witness the weigh-in. We decided, in fact, that we'd never be so stupid as to fish again in the winter and agreed not to join any more club expeditions till the summer. But when the coach eventually arrived back at Banstead, Fred Jones stood up in the gangway and addressed the club.

'It'll be the Thames at Caversham next time; January the eighteenth.'

Then he dropped his voice to a near whisper, lowered his head and looked straight at Dick and me.

'Big bream at Caversham – shoals of 'em.'

Fred Jones, electrician. He'd have made more

sparks as a politician or a con-man.
        'You can book us a seat now,' we said.

CHAPTER 4

The Deep Midwinter

I was warm from the car when I arrived at Ringwood and the north wind was very eager to greet me as I stood for a moment on the old town bridge to view the river. I hadn't put on my coat or gloves yet, and as I gauged the water level and tried to decide where to fish, my fingers began to tingle with the cold. Once out in the open fields, north of the town, the oncoming wind was like pliers on my face. The only good thing about it was that it blew away the incessant drone of the by-pass. I kept walking. Even though I was now well insulated I wanted to start fishing with my circulation working properly. The mud was like concrete and there were treacherous layers of ice in the flooded grass.

At the top of the fishery is a nice deep slack below

27

a willow, just the place for a chub. A chub was about the only fish I could expect to catch today and the good thing about the Avon at the moment is that the 'chavenders' are getting enormous. They may not exist in the vast shoals of forty years ago, but the average size is impressive – well over four pounds on some stretches, with individual specimens reaching seven or even eight pounds. I didn't want to be fiddling about with a float – anyway a static bait was probably the best option. So I set up a simple running leger, baited with bread crust on a size 6 hook and flicked the tackle into the slack.

Putting the rod in a rest, I sat on my creel and poured myself a steaming mug of black china tea laced with whisky. I was enjoying myself. The banks were deserted, the north wind had driven everything away except the redwings and fieldfares. There was an unreal intensity to the light, the landscape looked magical. Warm from my walk, sheltered from the wind by the willow, I sipped my tea and it tasted just fine. Good Lord! I was almost comfortable!

I have an angler's thermometer. A proper brass one. It's only used in extreme conditions, when I'm curious to learn if the fish were or were not biting when the temperature was either very low or very high. Today, after I'd plonked the thermometer in the river, it read 38°F, which is low, but above the level at which chub never feed. So my curiosity was satisfied and my optimism increased. If it had registered below 35°F I would have been more pessimistic.

But it would have been a challenge to catch a chub at such an unlikely low.

It really didn't matter what the thermometer said. The water was painfully cold. Just holding the wet string and wet brass casing in my fingerless mittens was like being scalded, and even as I was coiling it up, the string was becoming like wire, freezing in the sub-zero air. Down in those steely depths, in the cold press of the current, what were the fish feeling? How could they exist, let alone feed, on a day when even tractors stopped working because of frozen diesel?

The short afternoon began to show mellower colours as the sun slanted towards the south-west. I also moved south, fishing my way slowly downstream and not being so ridiculous as before when it seemed as if I was expecting a fish. I didn't search the eddies and slacks as thoroughly as I might, making only token casts so I could at least say I'd covered all the likely spots. But as the sun finally went down, I saw no point in prolonging my Arctic jaunt. Not only was the line constantly freezing to the rod rings, not only had my flasks of tea and whisky both been emptied, not only were my fingers completely numb and therefore unable to execute a proper cast, I had also sunk to that psychological level where even thinking is painful. When diesel freezes because of the wind chill then maybe the fluids in the brain also begin to freeze. Why else did the thought of someone painting the word 'Avocet' on my rod butt cause me such suffering? The idea of returning to the car and having to search in my pockets for a key was agonizing; then the thought that the lock would probably be frozen made me want to scream.

A swan drifted in silhouette between the reedbeds in front of me. Normally I dislike swans intensely. Such arrogant aggressive birds – just like humans. But there was something particularly elegant about this one, so black against the reflected sunset; I actually admired it. It hesitated and I wondered whether it was merely pausing for a piece of bread or waiting to take my spirit across the River Styx. It was joined by its mate and they soon got bored with me and disappeared into the twilight.

I'd had more than enough, but the image of the swans had acted like a sedative and I felt less brittle as I began to trudge back along the iron-hard banks. As I passed an anonymous-looking stretch of water which had no features to distinguish it from any other part of the river, everything suddenly became fluid in my head again. First the sedative, then this little shot of instinctive awareness working like anti-freeze. It was blindingly obvious that here was the place and this was the time and (though you will say, just as I can say in more reasonable moments, that it's easy to write such things in retrospect) it is these blips in the senses, these intervals of fluency, that lift you out of the ordinary and turn you into an absolute angler.

Five minutes after flicking a piece of flake into

the quiet underbank glide, the rod tip donked once, then pulled round and I was joined happily to a chub. There were some fierce downstream surges and I patiently eased rather than pulled, and eventually netted a fine portly specimen of around four-and-a-half pounds (I wasn't going to fiddle about with a spring balance). The furnace colours of the afterglow were bright on his flanks and he looked almost miraculous on the frosty grass.

I quickly slipped him back into his extra degrees, packed away the rod with no reservations and, on feet that could feel the ground again, headed back to the car where a well-licked key soon unfroze the doorlock.

As I drove home I realised I'd not only been lucky to catch a fish in such conditions, but it was fortunate that I had not frozen to the bank (as happened to a friend of mine once). I wouldn't be so daft as to go fishing in such conditions again.

Later, as I cradled a mug of hot tea beside a whispering stove, the phone rang. It was Mick and he wanted me to go chub fishing on the morrow.

'But the weather is cruel out there,' I said.

'So what?' he replied, 'it would just be good to be on the river. And because it has been so cold for so long the big fish are going to start feeding ravenously - any moment.'

'See you in the morning,' I said.

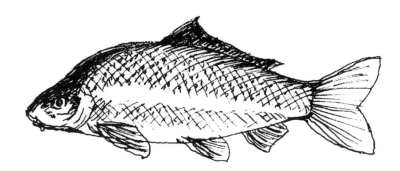

CHAPTER 5

Falling In

One of the most miraculous aspects of angling is the fact that most fishermen somehow manage to avoid the inevitable. They never – or almost never – fall in.

Yet think of the potential for it!

Fishing is an occupation that regularly draws millions of people to the very edge of precipitous and muddy and slippery banks or boggy unstable banks. They reach enthusiastically over the water with their rods, having no fear of the swirling depths below them, even when they occasionally stumble and splash a bit on hooking a good fish. Against such odds you would expect anglers to be spending almost as much time floundering in the river as fishing it, yet, I repeat, they never – or hardly ever – fall in.

There must be some powerful survival instinct that keeps them one step back from a dunking, though it would appear from their actions that they are indifferent to the dangers of even the most furious currents.

The only anglers who fall in are the very unlucky or careless ones, or the ones who take stupid risks.

I don't think of myself as being particularly unlucky or careless, though I do often take risks, especially if a large fish snags me, in which case I rarely hesitate before going in for it. Yet this is always a considered risk, a deliberate ducking rather than the accidental sort that I am writing about. I have fallen in though. I don't make a habit of it, but the sort of fishing I do makes the occasional big splash unavoidable.

Tree climbing, for instance, is a very good way to get a better view of the fish. But it can also lead to an unexpected closer view. Casting from a tree can get you right over the fish, but it can also get you right amongst them.

My first arboreal angling experience concerned the carp at my old village pond on Burgh Heath, in 1961. A great willow tree, its boughs spreading out both over and under the water, shaded nearly all of the eastern bank and provided the carp with an almost impenetrable sanctuary.

My friends and I would fish along the edge of the willows but we hardly ever made contact with anything and if we did, it was usually lost within moments as it dived unstoppably into the submerged boughs.

I decided that it would be a good idea if I actually fished from amongst these branches so that not only would I have the carp all round me, I could also drive them out of their cover if I hooked one. Once I'd struck a fish, I reckoned I could send it straight into open water simply by jumping up and down on my perch.

Waiting for what seemed like the perfect day – hot and calm and cloudless – I tackled up on the bank, using a seven foot solid fibreglass rod, Intrepid centrepin loaded with six pound line, porcupine quill and a size 6 hook. With the hook in the butt ring and everything wound up as taut as possible, I climbed up into the tree and slowly traversed from branch to branch, threading the rod between the fronds of leaves and being careful not to cause any sudden movement or vibration. It must have taken ten minutes to get into casting position, though of course I didn't have to cast at all but simply to lower the tackle between the boughs.

I'd chosen a spot where the branches were sparser than elsewhere and put the float down with the hook baited with flake, just a couple of yards from open water. Making myself as comfortable as possible on my branch, I prepared to wait all day if necessary.

I couldn't think of a more exciting place to fish. I was perched about five foot above the surface and I knew that almost every carp in the pond must be lurking unseen just below me. Now and then, a half submerged branch or shoot would tremble and shake as a fish nudged it in passing. Then, at other times, slow mysterious swirls would break up the green reflections. But despite all these signs of presence, my float never moved all morning and because I was getting cramped and stiff, I reeled up, left my rod in the branches, and swung ashore for some Tizer and tomato sandwiches.

My friends weren't even trying to fish for carp. They were having much more fun competing with each other for the number of perch and gudgeon they could catch before tea time and I was sorely tempted to stop monkeying around and join them.

Just one more hour, I thought, as I clambered back into the willow. I rebaited my hook, lowered it into the water and scattered a few free samples around it. Out in the open, the sun had been scorching and dazzling, but amongst the leaves it was cool and dark and it seemed even more promising than before. But why were the carp not interested in my bait?

I was on the brink of becoming bored by the look of my float. But then it stirred itself marvellously and I leant forward on the branch, thinking my suddenly thumping heart would certainly frighten the fish away. The float trembled and then simply sank straight down and I felt a deliciously energetic resistance when I struck. There was a splash and I was so excited I almost forgot the most important part of my plan.

Then I remembered and bounced up and down, the rod curving and shaking almost as much as the branch.

For a few seconds I couldn't tell in which direction the carp – it had to be a carp – was heading, but it didn't matter because after a few seconds more the bough broke with a loud crack and I went cracking and splashing into the pond.

I lost the fish, I lost my favourite float, I went down almost to my neck in black silt and when I staggered ashore my friends fell about laughing and said I looked like a sewer rat. But it was worth the effort, I thought – even though I'd only proved how daft it was to fish for carp from a tree.

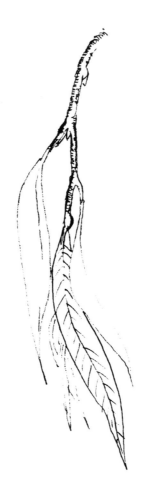

CHAPTER 6

Falling in Again

I first fished Redmire Pool in 1972 and quickly became familiar with all the best climbing trees around its banks. With a heron's eye view I would spend hours high above the water scanning the crystal clear depths for the mythical giants.

One afternoon, as I watched from the top of a tall alder, two common carp, one just under 20lb, the other maybe 35lb, materialised out of the weedbeds below me and began browsing right under the tree. I had some bait in my pocket, but I had to lower myself down carefully a few feet before I could see the fish clearly again and so observe their reactions to my offerings.

A dozen grains of sweetcorn were plopped round them and my heart quickened when they began to suck them up calmly from the bottom one after the other.

My rod was fifty yards down the bank, but it took me ages to climb down slowly without disturbing the fish and sneak off to get my gear. They were still there when I crept back, but I couldn't cast directly to them because there were too many branches between us. I realised the only sure way to present a bait was to get back up the tree and lower a hookful of corn straight onto their noses.

It was almost certain that the fish would vanish once I'd begun climbing again, but I pulled myself up through the branches and they remained drifting about close to the bank, actively searching out the last few grains. They seemed oblivious to me as I inched my way out along a bough and, exactly as I'd planned, lowered the bait into the water.

Like hounds sniffing out a bone, the carp slowly wove their course this way and that over the pale pool bed, picking up the odd morsel from between the sparse strands of weed. My cluster of corn was clearly visible – and then it wasn't visible at all and the line was slowly cutting through the surface, tightening up to the lowered rod tip.

The uproar when I struck was almost unbelievable

40

and even though I was perched high above the water the spray almost reached me. I was half lying along the branch, with the rod pointing down, and I wasn't prepared for the force of the carp's first rush. My balance wasn't secure and I was holding the rod with both hands so that when it wrenched round I was pulled straight out of the tree.

I fell awkwardly and almost horizontally into the water, but managed to keep the rod held out so that I didn't smash it beneath me. Even under the water I could hear the centre pin rasping – a sort of gurgling screech. But it wasn't deep, only a few feet, and I was soon upright again, with the rod bending nicely and a bow-wave cleaving the length of the pool.

It was a powerful fish, but it wasn't the big one. Wallowing and sploshing, I eventually steered it round the front of the tree where I'd left my net and so landed it. A beautiful fish: classically proportioned, deep bodied, sleek and brightly golden. It went just over sixteen pounds and was, I felt, worth the ducking.

Falling in is still easy: but landing the fish when you've had a ducking– now that is an acquired art.

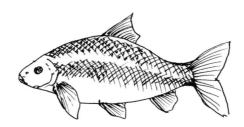

CHAPTER 7

The Lady of the Lake

Frustrated by our attempts to find the perfect carp pool, my brother Nick and I, together with friends Graham and Guy, had begun sampling the less-than-perfect gravel pit fishing of north-west Kent. Actually, the fishing was quite good, but we weren't so keen on the semi-urban surroundings, the lack of atmosphere and the sometimes crowded banks. It was a world away from the dream we were still looking for - the remote, neglected lake on some abandoned estate, haunted only by ghosts and enormous, mind-boggling carp.

After a particularly dodgy night at Horton Kirby, which may have been a well-known carp water but was also, after dark, the setting for all kinds of other dubious activities, we felt we must make more effort to track down our own ideal pool. And after a week or two of searching, Guy came rushing round to our house to say he'd found the perfect place. A rich friend of his mother's had recently moved into a house, the garden of which ran right down to the banks of an old lake. Someone had fished there only the previous week and, in one night, had caught seventeen carp. That was more carp than the four of us had caught in our entire lives.

To round off this mouth-watering story, Guy said that, after exhaustive negotiations, with his mother acting as mediator, permission had been granted for us all to fish there the very next night. The usual conditions would apply: no noise, no lights, no fireworks and every fish to be returned.

Horton Kirby, Brooklands and all the other desolate pits began to recede back into the darkness and a new watery glow began to flood our imaginations.

The introduction to the place was even better than our imaginations. We got down to the house, near Betchworth, Surrey, at around seven in the evening. Our benefactor led us onto a lawn which ran down to the water's edge. The pool was about three acres, with a wood on the opposite bank. There were reeds and lilies and a large fallen tree, half-submerged, reaching towards us from the far side - the perfect roost for carp and only a thirty-yard cast from the lawn.

We set up our rods, tossed some mashed bread towards the tree as an attractor and made our casts, using flake as bait. As we settled down on our deck-chairs, the saintly lady re-appeared with a tray of toast and coffee -

something our dream had definitely lacked. She asked us if we could keep 'one or two' fish in the net so she could see them in the morning before we released them. Then she wished us good fishing and goodnight and left us chortling to ourselves on the bank.

The July night came on slowly enough for us to add all kinds of extravagant details to our already ambitious hopes. If one angler - a trout fisherman, at that - could extract seventeen carp in a night, surely we were going to catch fifty. And how big were they going to be? Ten? Twenty? Thirty pounders?

At around eleven o'clock, when there was still a vague glow in the north-west sky, Graham's indicator began to move. The silver foil on his line rose slowly from the grass to the butt ring and he leaned forward and struck.

We all held our breath, waiting for a violent rush or a great splash, but Graham just said, 'Well, it's a fish,' and began reeling it steadily in. There was more of a splish than a splash when it came under the bank and he lifted out something silvery - a roach of about a pound.

We reasoned that there were bound to be other species besides carp in the lake, but as the night progressed we began to wonder whether the carp would ever get a look in. Every few minutes someone's indicator would rise up and the resultant strike would produce another roach.

Fifty fish, we had envisaged. By bleary sunrise we must have landed a hundred. Some of them were quite large for roach, certainly larger than the ones we normally caught in rivers, when we occasionally fished for them. But now we never wanted to see another roach again for as long as we lived.

To please our lady of the lake, however, we had kept the two biggest fish - roach of around one and a half pounds - in a keep-net and when she eventually appeared again we showed them to her.

'Carp are such lovely fish,' she said, gently touching their silver scales.

CHAPTER 8

Sacred Water

As you may hazily remember from those wonderfully sleep-inducing history lessons, almost half the country used to be owned by the Church until, sometime in the 16th century, along came Henry the Eighth who decided the church had too much power. In a fit of pique he knocked down several abbeys and dispossessed the Church of most of its property.

Think of all those well-stocked stew ponds, full of perch, pike and wild carp where the monks used to fish. Suddenly they were all owned by the Crown, which makes me wonder whether old Henry was an angler as well as a tyrant. Actually, they were not all put under Crown ownership; many monasteries and abbeys survived Henry's wrath and the brothers were able to continue fishing in the moats and ponds for their traditional Friday fish.

I mention this because I've always had a soft spot for monastery stew ponds. I like the slightly haunted atmosphere that hangs over these historic waters; I like the appearance of them, especially the Gothic architecture that often surrounds them; but best of all I like the wild carp, a fish that is always associated with them. In fact the wild carp is my favourite fish – a creature so much more elegant, spirited and fastidious than his portly relation, the 'king' carp.

Knowing my fascination with holy waters, a friend of mine, Algy Selwood, told me he had some inside information for me.

'What do you mean?' I asked him.

'You remember I married a rector's daughter,' he said. 'Well, it seems that the rector has discovered a secret lake owned by the church and he's going on holiday there. What's more, he's invited us to go, too.'

'I didn't know your father-in-law was an angler,' I said.

'He's not,' said Algy. 'The reason he's going is because there's a holiday cottage on the bankside specifically for members of the church and their families.'

'Are there any carp?' I asked.

'According to my father-in-law the lake is well stocked with "big fish".'

Sacred Water

It all sounded very promising. An old lake on church property, only accessible to churchmen and their families, containing large fish that were almost certainly carp. Naturally Algy would take his rod and report back to me. If things turned out well, I'd be invited up for a day as their guest. And if things looked really exciting I'd get hold of a white dog collar, pretend I was the local vicar and pitch a tent on the bankside for a week.

Come August, the phone rang one evening and it was a breathless and very excited Algy. 'There are dozens and dozens of them, carp, basking in the lily pads all day!' he said. 'I've tried, but I can't catch them. Some of them are huge. You must come and have a go. We all want to see if you can catch one.'

I'd been planning to go carp fishing that night anyway, with another friend, Rick Ford, so my old van was all packed, ready to go.

'Is it OK if the guest brings a guest?' I asked, cheekily. 'It's just that Rick was all set to come fishing with me at this very moment.'

'He can be gillie,' said Algy.

It was a hundred and fifty miles to the church lake and with Algy's directions, a dark night and a maze of country lanes, we took five hours to get there. Dawn was just breaking as we drove through a line of dark trees and saw a pale expanse of water in front of us. There was the cottage, as Algy had described, standing at the lake's edge.

49

It had a wooden veranda, like a landing stage, built on piers above the water. The banks were marshy and dense with reeds and Algy had said the best place to fish was from the veranda, especially as he had tea and toast in constant supply. This being so, he'd baited the area heavily with mashed bread and as he'd so vividly explained on the phone, the carp had burst through the lily beds and onto the groundbait 'like a pack of dogs'! Yet he hadn't been able to catch one, or even get a bite.

Rick and I crept silently onto the veranda, our rods already tackled up. We'd decided to float-fish with sweetcorn, using 8lb line, right at the edge of the lilies. It was a lovely looking lake, almost exactly as Algy had described, though, at about three acres, it was smaller than we'd expected. It smelt of fish – a faint, sweet, peppery smell that I always associate with old carp ponds. However, as I stood on the veranda and took a deep breath, I realised this fishy aroma was stronger than I'd expected. Perhaps, I thought, it was the very still, damp air before sunrise, but the lake smelt like an old keepnet. 'It must be stuffed with fish,' said Rick.

Naturally, the cottage was silent and Algy would probably be asleep till 9 o'clock, along with everyone else, which meant we'd have four hours uninterrupted fishing. He'd obviously fished till well into the night, waiting for us to show up. His rod was leaning against the wooden rail on the veranda and the landing net was still dry.

50

It was still only just light, enough to see our floats when we cast out, but as the light increased we suddenly realised the water in front of us was a mass of bubbles. Furthermore, the bubbles were still rising. My float twitched, bobbed and sat quietly again. The rod had been lying on the wooden boards, but now I carefully picked it up as the float again curtsied and then slid decisively away towards the patch of lilies.

The strike didn't produce the expected result. Instead of a violent surge into the pads, there was just a feeble flapping and tugging and then a slow swirl on the surface. This was no high-powered wild carp and I steadily reeled in a very dark coloured bream of about 3lb. Then Rick's float sank slowly from sight and he too hauled in a bream. Like my fish, it seemed half asleep – but then most still-water bream never become fully alive and spend most of their lives semi-comatose.

'Fine carp lake you've brought me to!' snorted Rick as he hooked another bream next cast.

'Early days yet,' I reasoned. 'Plenty of time to get amongst the proper fish.'

The sun rose above the trees. The early mist disappeared and the ducks and moorhens began to splash about. Our floats continued to slide away under the surface and the bream continued to feed enthusiastically on whatever we threw at them. Eventually I hooked something that felt more solid, more substantial, and for a moment I thought

I'd actually got hold of a real carp. But then it suddenly gave up and came wallowing and plunging into the net – the best and the smelliest of the day, a bream of nearly 6lb.

If we hadn't come so far with such high expectations we might have enjoyed ourselves, but as it was, we were a little disappointed. However, breakfast on the veranda, with the rector and Algy, was splendid, even though we were interrupted several times by the slow departure of our floats, and even though the toast tasted of fish slime.

'I take it these bream were a slight case of mistaken identity?' enquired Rick.

'Well,' said Algy apologetically, 'they looked exactly like carp to me when they were basking in the pads.'

'Tell me,' I said, over another pot of tea, 'how come you never caught a bream, though you spent all yesterday fishing with the same baits we're using now?'

'Simple,' replied Algy. 'I was only fishing for carp.'

CHAPTER 9

The Miracle of a Best Fish

Even when you have been fishing for a lifetime you still get a little surge of jubilation if you suddenly catch another personal best. When you are young and daft, though, a best fish is a matter not just of joy, but of serious importance, a symbol of achievement. And it's better still when such an event is shared with an angling companion as, apart from anything else, it proves you didn't dream it.

I remember, for instance, catching a best perch when I was fourteen. Had not three friends been fishing with me, I don't think anyone would have believed me because, in those days, none of us had ever caught anything over a pound in all our short lives. Yet this fish was an incredible one pound and a half.

Derek, Dave, Mike and I were fishing the Thames at Kingston and enjoying ourselves catching bleak, one after the other. It didn't matter that they were small and insignificant; the fact that our floats were being nicked under every cast made them hugely worthwhile. But in the middle of our tiddler snatching, Derek's rod suddenly went over into an incredible bend. In those days any bend that wasn't caused by a snag or an overhanging branch was incredible. We all stared aghast at the quivering arc – and then fell around laughing when the rod boinged straight again, though Derek didn't laugh at all. Whatever it was had broken his line.

'I was reeling in a bleak', he said, 'and something grabbed it!' Pike? Perch? Thames trout? Barracuda?

The next time we cast and hooked a bleak, we let it scurry around on the surface until it just lay in the ripples like a floating silver leaf. But nothing monstrous rose again from the depths. We presumed, therefore, that Derek's brief encounter had been one of those angling miracles that only happen once in a lifetime – and he'd botched it. Yet there was no doubt that, for the next few hours, there was a novel sense of drama about our fishing. After all, whatever it had been was still down there somewhere...

Sometime during the afternoon I went for a wander upstream and came upon a group of very excited anglers who were just lowering a keep-net into the river. I asked if I could have a look at their catch and was proudly shown an amazing perch of well over a pound.

'Cor!' I said. 'What did you get it on?'

'Legered dead bleak.'

I hurried back downstream, described what I'd beheld to my three friends, took the float off my line and replaced it with a half-ounce coffin lead. Then I stole the next bleak that was caught, tapped it on the head, hooked it on my line and plopped it into our swim.

Of course no one seriously believed that anything exciting was going to happen to me. We had, in the past, managed to tease out all kinds of wondrous angling lore from the few successful fishermen we knew (successful as in 'anglers who not only owned but even used landing nets'). Yet nothing that had been divulged to us ever made any difference to our catches. It was true that our hopes had once been raised to such a peak by some revelatory gem that I'd even saved up and bought a landing net. But the secret additive to our baits did not bring the net into action.

Perhaps twenty minutes passed in which I had to sit still and pretend to be expectant while my three friends continued to happily harvest the bleak shoals. Then Dave got a roach! It must have been all of six inches long. Another five minutes, I thought, and then I'll put the float back on. But I didn't have to wait that long. My rod was in the rest one moment and suddenly out of it the next, the tip having been wrenched round and down and the whole lot then clattering along the bank. When I grabbed it I could hardly believe the sensation of solid but living resistance. It was a fish! A real stonking fish!

In those days we nearly always used fixed spool reels and always screwed the clutch down tight – just in case the unbelievable happened. We never believed what the text books advised: that a heavy fish should be allowed to run. If we ever hooked a heavy fish we weren't going to give it an inch. Therefore we were witness to a double miracle. The first was that I'd actually hooked a big fish. The second was that my line didn't break.

The monster dived with such force that everything, including me, was stretched out like a thin elastic band just before it snaps. Rod and line seemed to chime together like a tinny bell, but then, astonishingly, the pressure began to ease and the fish came round in a circle towards us.

'Whoar!' yelled someone. 'Look at that!'

'It's a perch!' stammered someone else. 'I can s-see the s-s-stripes!'

Winding and walking backwards at the same time, I hauled the great fish over the landing net. We all gathered round it, marvelling at its colours, its spines, its stripes, its immensity. I had to keep looking at it to make sure it was real. And I had to look at my friends to make sure they knew it was real too.

'This is great!' said Dave 'Now we know how to

catch big perch!'

Predictably, we all began fishing with dead bleak after that. And, in days to come, we tried sprats and little silver spinners. But we never caught another large Thames perch again.

CHAPTER 10

A Double Miracle

It was early season and Alex (9), Will (6) and I went down to some carp ponds I knew near Wimborne. We'd fished there before the previous year and both boys had caught fish up to 2lb, which, when I was their age, would have seemed a stunning achievement. But Alex and Will are already a bit blasé about such ordinary rod benders. Both boys have already seen rather too many large fish in their lives to think there is anything unusual about them. In fact William's first outing into the wide world, when he was less than a week old, was to the Hampshire Avon where he was 'slimed' by a barbel twice as big as him.

However, though they have both caught many more rod benders than I had at their age (I hadn't caught any!) their largest specimens to date were a four-pounder to Alex and a three-pounder to Will.

William chose the upper pool, on the edge of a wood, and began to float fish with a bunch of maggots and a new hollow glass boy's rod that our friend Mick Canning had given him. Alex had crept off to the more overgrown pool deep in the wood. He too was fishing with maggots under a float and he also had a new rod that Mick had just given him – a vintage split cane Lucky Strike, made by Allcock in the 1950s.

Within minutes of casting, Will's float began to bob about enthusiastically, but we knew it wasn't a carp testing the bait. The pool is stream-fed and full of ravenous minnows and we had learnt that the most encouraging thing your float can do there is to sit very still. The minnows are constantly tweaking at even the largest bunch of maggots, but as soon as a carp comes on the prowl they run and hide and there follows a wonderfully intense period of calm which usually ends with the float sliding smoothly away.

After half an hour of pathetic trembling and bobbing William's float suddenly became static. In fact there was something menacing about the way it just sat there, so motionless, so expectant. There was a slight furling on the surface, then the yellow tip went down in one decisive movement and, with a shout and a big splash, Will had connected with a carp. A good one, too. It dived into the lily bed on his right, got stuck, but was gradually eased free and after several slow passes and heavy swirls, I got the net under it.

William had landed not only his best ever carp, but his best ever fish: a mirror of 6lb 6oz. He looked at it lovingly, but also a little incredulously, as if it was a conjuror's trick that was going to vanish as magically as it had appeared. He laid his hand gently on it, not only to feel the strange leathery flank, but also to confirm its reality.

We took some photographs and William was obviously very pleased with himself, if a little unsure as to how he was going to tell his elder brother and greatest hero that he had just out-carped him. A few minutes after the fish had been slid back into its home we heard a distant shout from the wood.

'Net!' yelled a familiar voice. 'Bring a net!'

We dashed into the trees, net at the ready, and after a minute came upon the big brother doing battle with what appeared to be another quite big carp. Alex had hooked it in a little bay by the inlet stream and said he'd even seen it as it first approached the bait. When he hooked it, it just ploughed straight through a dense weedbed towards the island in the pool's centre.

In my boyhood, anything making a serious bid for freedom like that was almost instantly lost, so convinced was I in the 'hit and hold' method. But Alex realised long ago that it's better to give a little before you take a little.

He also understands the advantages of a centrepin over a fixed spool in a tight corner. So although there were a few tense moments, with the carp bundling itself up in weedstems or suddenly shooting away at high speed across a clear stretch of water, Alex didn't have to strain the line overmuch and the old cane rod stood the test nicely.

Eventually, I leaned out with the net and he brought a fine common carp into the mesh.

And not just fine, but remarkable, because when we weighed it, it was exactly 6lb 6oz.

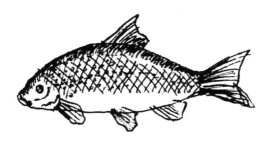

CHAPTER 11

Spate

Every month a man from the National Rivers Authority (now renamed the Environment Agency) used to come knocking on my door. He wasn't interested in the validity of my rod licence; all he wanted to do was to check the level of my well.

Every cottage in this village has its own well, each one dug by hand centuries ago through a hundred feet of solid chalk; but for some reason mine is the only Tollard Royal well. It's all part of a detailed survey of all the catchment area of the River Allen, a pretty chalk stream that eventually flows into the Dorset Stour. When he plumbed the depths recently, the inspector found that the water level in my well was 60ft below ground. In October 1994, one of the wettest months in recorded history, it rose some 20 feet. After years of low rainfall and shrunken rivers, we seemed to be heading for a time when we'd be swopping our cars for boats. There had been enough rain to inspire a whole empire of ark builders. I had never seen the river so high in late autumn – and that year all our local winterbourns had started running three months early.

Anglers suffer mixed reactions when their favourite rivers start to rise. If the water colours quickly and thickly it can often put the fish right off, but on a predominantly clear chalk stream like the Hampshire Avon, the fish can get quite lively. Some of my best ever catches of barbel were made as the Avon was about to burst its banks. The main problem once the surrounding fields begin to flood is not finding the fish, but finding the river!

I went over to Ibsley the other week and was presented with the magnificent sight of hundreds of acres under water. Woods and willow clumps had become islands. Field boundaries were defined as rows of half submerged fence posts, each post forming a long trailing bow-wave in the surprisingly powerful flow. The swans, gulls and other waterfowl were having a wonderful time and there was a cormorant chasing something along a flooded ditch, a quarter of a mile from the main river. I had this wild idea that if I could wade across a couple of meadows I could reach a big bend where, even in this flood, there'd be a large area of slack water jam-packed with feeding barbel.

Of course I wouldn't even have attempted this dangerous mission had I not been very familiar with the surrounding country. But I knew the courses of sidestreams and ditches and remembered the positions of depressions and hollows in the fields. It was still a fairly crazy thing to do, especially as there was no one else for miles around; but I enjoy the occasional challenge, all the more so if this includes the chance of a monster fish.

After a very poor start, the barbel fishing has been spectacular this season and I guessed the turmoil of this flood had roused the giants from their deep sanctuary. I parked my car on some high ground and, donning waders, strode off with my tackle along a flooded path. It was surprisingly heavy going as even the most gentle dip in the path meant the water washed dangerously high. But tracks and paths lie generally lower than their surroundings and I knew I'd rise up in the water when I was out in the open fields. There was a little bridge ahead, visible only as two parallel rows of brickwork poking above the surface. On either side was the course of the Harbidge Stream, normally a shallow, reedy trickle, now a place where the floodwaters boiled noticeably and abruptly deepened, from two to ten feet. Once over the bridge, I felt safer and headed out across the open fields like a ferry just out if its harbour. I made an impressive wave as I slogged slowly along, but though I recalled the whereabouts of ditches and depressions I was wary about such things as rabbit holes and collapsing mole runs.

Though the prospect of fishing was uppermost in my mind, it didn't completely cloud my sense of survival and I kept close to the reassuring lines of the fences. If I tripped and went under, I could easily pull myself up again, holding on to the wire. Ahead of me was a half-drowned copse where, in normal conditions, the river took a big loop and where, even in a flood, there was always a quiet backflow along the upstream part of the bend. Also, there was a little wooden fisherman's bench on a bit of high bank and I could just see the top half of it as I crossed a submerged stile. The bench was the precise fishing spot I'd had in mind, for I'd often sat on it in near flood conditions in the past and had regularly tempted large barbel from the deep slack next to it.

A just visible reed bed made a useful demarcation line between the gently flowing floodwater on my side and the deep, riotous torrent on the other. Where there were no reeds or bankside trees there was still a fairly clearly defined crease between the two different flows. But the slack by the bench was as quiet as normal and I flicked a hookful of luncheon meat into it. I thought I'd get an immediate response. There was almost certainly a great shoal of porpoise-sized barbel down there. Within seconds I'd hook one of them and, after towing me downstream for half a mile, the fish would come up over the bank and race off across the flooded fields. I'd have to dive under the fences to follow it. But I didn't get a bite first or second or even third cast. Heavy cloud came over and once again it began to rain torrentially. A fleet of swans drifted behind me, like yachts on a grey sea. In front of me a whole tree went bumping and pirouetting down the main river, followed sometime later by an old wooden door. There was a continual stream of the usual floodwater jetsam – fertiliser bags, drink cans, wooden posts, plastic bottles. And just before dusk, wreathed by uprooted brambles, a dead and waterlogged sheep sailed solemnly past.

Suddenly, I felt a tug on the line – it didn't seem like a barbel bite and I had a horrid suspicion that – it tugged again – yes, it was only an eel. I had two more and wished I'd brought some sweetcorn.

Then I noticed that the water level was rising again. It was almost up and over the bench and, looking back over my shoulder, the nearest high ground seemed rather further away than before.

'Idiot!' I said to myself, winding in and chucking all my gear in the creel. Using my landing net pole as a wading staff, I surged back towards the almost submerged parapet on the little bridge. It was strenuous work against the enormous southerly push of water and I wondered whether Ibsley Weir, a mile up the valley, had been breached. But, apart from a soaking from perspiration, I made it back without even filling a wader.

CHAPTER 12

Flood

As I write, the valley outside my window is grey with frost and the last leaves are falling in ones and twos from my apple tree. Winter is finally here and it looks lovely and blue and clean. And yet I'm still a little disturbed, because although the wheels of the seasons are turning at last, there is still no sign of rain.

Of course, we have had some rain, but compared to last November there is still a drought in the south of

England and it's not much better up north. For the first time in its history my well is dry in the autumn. However, it was low this time last year and then, a month before Christmas, the rain suddenly began. First it was just a few wet days and nights, and then came a deluge as momentous as Noah's flood.

I remember my last fishing trip of '94, looking for the line of the river in an overflowing valley. There were thousands of acres under water. All the weir hatches down the Avon were wide open and the river stormed through with a thunderous roar. But I guessed there were big barbel to be had in the few more sheltered stretches, where now immensely deep eddies had formed on the inside of bends, or where sidestreams provided refuge from the violent currents. The water was so coloured in those early days of the flood that you just couldn't see where the fields ended and the river began. One false step and you'd end up in Christchurch Harbour.

Naturally, there was no one else foolish enough to be fishing on that day and I had an oceanic river all to myself. I waded along a path and reached a place where only the trees gave any clue as to the precise edge of the bank. But I know that bit of river like the back of my reel, so keeping well back from the places where I remembered the bank to be undercut, I cast a rolling leger into the quietest part of the run.

The bait was luncheon meat and after about half

70

an hour, I had a quick jag of a take which was definitely chubish rather than barbelish. Scaling down to a smaller snick of meat produced nothing. Rebaiting with a great chunk the size of a tangerine resulted in a firm pull, the rod tip actually bending before I struck. Yes, I thought, definitely chubish, though the deep water made it feel initially much more substantial than it was. Just over 4lb.

Then the rain began again. The sky darkened and seemed to descend onto my hat so that the brim became like a gutter that overflowed round my shoulders and down my back. The great thing about a long waterproof trench coat is that as long as you wear a big hat and waders, the rain just can't get through to you and you end up laughing at it. But the rain became so torrential that no matter how waterproof my coat, I knew it wouldn't stop me from drowning. The flood would rise still further, the paths and even the footbridges across the ditches would submerge still deeper and I'd be cut off completely. Perhaps I'd even have to spend the night at the top of the tree. So I splashed hurriedly home without recasting.

The weather over Christmas was quite cold. January began cold, then just became wetter and wetter. There were flood warnings on almost every major river and at the beginning of February the radio announced that the Hampshire Avon was at Red Alert. During the cold spell, I'd not had any hankering to get back to the river or anywhere else watery. The only fish that feeds well in sub-zero temperatures is the grayling, and my local grayling river was still over its banks, even before the deluge began once again.

But the Avon's Red Alert coincided with a week of exceptionally mild weather and I knew that if I could just find where the barbel were I'd catch one. There was a favourite floodwater swim that I remembered down on the Royalty Fishery. I hadn't cast there for a year or two, but in the past it had always fished best when the rest of the river was virtually inaccessible. So, as the rain turned the roads into canals and the roundabouts into ponds, I drove down to Christchurch and found the Avon higher and broader than I'd ever seen it before. Though the level could probably never rise over the steep west bank, the water's edge on the eastern side was suddenly half a mile away. The Royalty looked like a vast lake with a curiously boiling margin. Typically, my floodwater swim was occupied by the only other angler on the river. I was going to push him in, but then I realised it was a friend of mine, Ron Smith and he rather surprised me by saying he'd been there for four hours and hadn't had a single bite.

'But the barbel were feeding well the other day,' he said. 'I had four to 9lb last Tuesday afternoon!'

'This is Friday though,' I said. 'And my first trip of 1995, so I've got to find a barbel feeding somewhere.'

Ron reeled in and we wandered down the bank, looking for a quiet eddy or slack, out of the turbulent current. We came to a promising-looking spot, a narrow strip of calm water formed by a jutting shoulder of reedy bank. I knew there was a deep hole right next to this slack – now an even deeper hole – and everything about it felt just perfect. As Ron chatted about his New Year's fishing, I tackled up with a lissome 11-foot carp rod (a Barder *Bishop*), my 1922 Aerial, 8lb line and a 1oz running leger. Bait was a very greasy kind of luncheon meat on a size 6. I simply dropped the tackle under the rod tip and felt it slowly sink to the gravel bed, ten or twelve feet below.

'First cast of the year,' I said happily. Sitting on my creel, well back from the water's edge, we began to discuss the astonishing state of the river. Five minutes passed, no more, and then the tip of the rod twitched and wobbled and I struck. We both burst out laughing.

'It's Boris!' chuckled Ron. 'Boris the barbel on your first cast!'

The way the rod stayed fixed in a trembling curve convinced us it could be nothing else, but there was also nothing yet to persuade me this was a particularly big Boris. Just the usual satisfyingly concentrated resistance, holding low to the river bed, but with no mad rushes into the main current. However, I wasn't converting it to my way of thinking. If I gained a yard, it took it back, time and time again. Now and then a more determined effort meant that I lowered the rod tip easing the pressure and this always dissuaded the fish from continuing into the heavy surge. I didn't want to have the fish sweeping with the strong current towards the railway bridge, only a hundred yards downstream, and I managed to keep teasing it back into the safety of the slack. About ten minutes passed. Then the line's angle was more vertical than diagonal and I raised the barbel momentarily into mid-water. Down he went again, deep and slow, but I knew then that he was going to see the light of day.

The next moment we saw him, six or seven feet below the surface, looking dark gold and quite impressive. The lazy slosh of his tail sounded wonderful and ponderous as I eased the fish over the net, and as soon as Ron lifted we knew it was over ten pounds - a very deep bodied, extremely portly, gloriously coloured, barbel which pulled the balance to ten pounds ten ounces. I suddenly realised the rain had stopped and for a moment it actually seemed as if the clouds might break. But it was merely a final brief blessing from Izaak for me to savour the marvellous fish properly before the heavens opened once again.

I packed up at dark and drove home up the east side of the river, via Sopley, Ringwood and Ibsley. When I turned across the Avon at Ibsley Bridge I was confronted by a 'Road Closed, Flood' sign. The road formed a causeway across the water meadows between the river and Harbridge Stream and, in previous wet winters, I'd regularly seen it drowned. Even without a warning sign most cars refused when they came up to it, but a diesel (with its lack of electrics) doesn't care about water and my old Peugeot always chugged straight through without even a splutter. I know it was dark and I couldn't see the depth in front of me, but I was buoyed up by my catch and felt positively invincible. For a hundred yards there were only puddles, then the road disappeared under a dark acreage of water the depth of which was indicated by the two lines of fence posts leading towards Harbridge. It didn't look too bad and for a while the car burbled on uncomplaining until I realised the water was becoming not only deeper than I'd expected, but deeper on one side than the other! This wasn't because of any camber or gutter, but because of the powerful southerly flow – right to left. I glanced through the side window to see the glow from Fordingbridge reflected in a moving sea of floodwater. Furthermore, I could see the bow-wave I was making and even hear the lap-lapping against the door as the level rose steadily higher on my off-side.

There was no possibility of stopping and reversing, or just stopping. I was in that desperate yet exultant mentality that refuses to recognise any direction but forward, even if forward leads to disaster. The headlight beams began to turn greenish as the water came up round the bonnet and I remembered that a diesel engine will always keep going unless the air intake becomes flooded. Another three inches I guessed. The current was so strong against my right side, it seemed I'd be swept away any moment.

The car strained a little, even in first, as if it was going up a very steep incline. The fence posts were just visible on either side, but I still felt like a submariner about to dive. I noticed the broken water on my left, where the fast flow coming across the road hit the slower deeps along the fence-line. I could even hear it above the engine drone and exhaust bubble – a steady, threatening, rushing sound. But the headlights gradually grew brighter as the bonnet rose up above water level again and the amphibious vehicle brought me safely into Harbridge.

Had I blanked on the Royalty and therefore made the voyage with a less fervent, less defiant spirit, would I perhaps have suffered a moment's fateful hesitation? The waters will always part for the captor of a big fish!

CHAPTER 13

A Stinging Loss

I always enjoyed the long walk upstream from the bridge. It had become not only familiar but also occasionally surprising. My fishing on that stretch of the River Mole normally began at the top of the fishery and slowly meandered back down to the bridge - an exercise that could take either a whole day or maybe just a couple of hours, depending on my mood and the mood of the fish.

The walk up to the boundary, however, always took roughly the same amount of time as I would only ever glance into my favourite pools and glides and never cast into them. I would be in too much haste to reach the best pool of all - a place that was always overlooked by everyone else but which produced more big perch and chub than anywhere else I'd fished along the entire river. Furthermore, I'd seen a monster there, a chub that could easily have weighed over eight pounds.

So though I'd often glimpse other biggish fish on my quarter of a mile walk along the tree-hung bank, I wouldn't be tempted until I'd first investigated the Ash Tree Pool.

However, one day I broke with tradition. I was half-way up to the boundary and had just rounded a bend where there was always a shoal of roach and dace, when I spotted another tremendous chub. It wasn't as big as the original giant, but I reckoned it was six pounds.

The resident roach and dace didn't seem to mind the fact that this great chevin had come to visit them. The riverbed was pale and sandy beneath them and the chub appeared like a black-tailed airship floating through a formation of small grey kites.

A few yards downstream was a spreading bramble bush and I reckoned I could use that as cover, crouching behind it and casting a big slug up into the shoal. It looked almost straightforward and I was actually quite surprised to find a large chub in such an accessible position. If I landed it, it would not only be my best-ever chub but also my biggest-ever fish of any species.

Quickly, I assembled my three piece eleven footer, clamped on an Intrepid Deluxe reel and ran the 6lb line through the rings. My tackle and technique for chub and perch was now always the same in summer. A size 6 hook baited with either slug or lobworm, and never any lead or float. The simplest methods, I'd discovered, were the most effective.

I crawled into position, waited a minute so that I might merge better into my background, then cast a long line beyond the shoal. The slug landed with a bit of splash, but I'd learned that chub can somehow tell the difference between a slug entering water and a float or a lead. While they would always flee from the latter, they would sometimes charge forwards to grab the former. Of course there was no danger of even the biggest roach in the shoal tackling the slug. Even a three pound roach couldn't manage it and there was nothing in the shoal half that size.

As the bait came drifting back through midwater towards me, so the chub swerved out of the shoal towards it. I couldn't see exactly what happened next, but the line jagged across the surface, then continued to float downstream. The chub sidled back amongst the roach and I reeled in to find a severely chomped slug dribbling from the hook.

Drat! I should've struck!

The next cast produced no response at all and I guessed the old chavender was wise to my ploy. But he didn't seem disturbed and I wasn't impatient or frustrated. I simply sat and waited, quite happy to spend half an hour in forced stillness and contained anticipation. There was nothing in the world I would rather have done.

When I could bear it no longer, I took a deep breath and made a third attempt, my slow casting action lessening the botch-potential. The bait didn't fly far enough, but the splash from behind him fooled the chub completely. He turned and went straight for it, his white

79

lips positively flashing as he engulfed it. He turned and there was another brighter flash as I set the hook.

There was a large bed of cabbages (underwater lilies) downstream and the fish swept straight towards it, towing me along the bank behind it. I floundered alongside the front of a bramble bush, getting a bootful of water as I tried to avoid the worst of the thorns and then nearly falling in completely when a patch of underbank grass turned out to be growing on a raft of flotsam. With the rod almost looped, I scrambled up onto firm ground and put my foot straight onto a wasp's nest. The insects took offence and within moments an angry swarm was screaming all round me.

I waved my arms frantically to keep the wasps off my face and the chub continued to heave. The combined effect worked perfectly in our favour. The line broke, leaving the chub free to dive deep into the cabbages and me free to dash far away across the fields.

CHAPTER 14

A Sting in the Tail

There were five of us spread out along a half-mile stretch of the River Avon at Bisterne. Edward Barder, famous for his pressed nodes, was up at the boundary; Shaun Linsley, who was trying out his first split-cane rod, was fishing the oak tree hole; Mick Canning, who has caught more big Avon barbel than any other angler I know, was fishing the pot; Roy Chatfield who could tease out a fish on the most unlikely day, was casting off High Bank; I was sitting in the salmon hut enjoying a cup of tea.

   We had been on the river since lunchtime, but it was now six o'clock and no-one, not even Roy, had even tweaked a barbel. The weather was warm and calm and the blue of the sky had that pale luminous quality that you will only ever find in September. There was also a kind of timelessness in the air, it being so still and uneventful, yet the sun was descending towards the distant hills, telling me that tea-time must now end.

Whatever the fishing has been like during the day, you are almost guaranteed it will be better as the sun goes down, especially if you are after barbel.

I put away the tea things, baited my hook with four grains of corn and went back to the deep run in the weedbeds where I'd been fishing all afternoon.

There were definitely barbel in the swim - or, at least, one barbel. A fish had rolled on the surface not long after my first cast. But all I'd caught during the afternoon was a two-pound chub.

The river takes a big sweep from south to west just there and so the whole of that length simply ignites when the sun goes down, like a fuse touched by a flame. And you hang onto the rod with a little more expectancy, waiting for the explosive thud of a barbel bite. But the more I waited, the more nothing happened.

I was snapped out of my reverie by Mick who crept down to tell me that Roy had just had a brace, five and eight pounds.

'There's a shoal of barbel at the upstream end of High Bank', he said. 'You can see them when they drift out from the weed streamers.'

Despite my sense of anticipation, I left my swim to have a look. The sight of barbel in the river is almost as good as a barbel in the net. Roy was looking even more pleased with life than usual and he pointed towards the dark shapes of the fish as they ghosted out of a bed of midstream ranunculus and then dropped gently downstream, de-materialising into the reflected afterglow.

82

Roy insisted that Mick move up and have a cast, the inevitable result of which was a well bent Wallis Wizard.

'Strewth!' was Mick's only comment. It was a powerful fish and after twice weaving itself through the weedbeds and being coaxed out again it made a splendid rush downstream and almost got below the big oak that leans out across the river. Mick persuaded it in under the bank, but the current was faster there and the barbel refused to be drawn back against it.

Though the bank was heavily overgrown with willow herb and nettles at the tail of the swim, I grabbed the net, pushed through the stems and lowered myself down, scrabbling about with my feet until I found a bit of firm gravel beneath the marginal rushes. There was the fish, wallowing just within reach, but as I brought the net up around it so a furious buzzing rose up around my head. I'd obviously kicked open a wasp's nest.

I heaved the landing net up, raised the handle over my head and yelled for Roy to grab it. As the irate insects swarmed over me I thought for a moment that I should simply dive in the river - but it looked a bit treacherous in the half dark. In less time than it takes to say 'sting' I was back on firm ground, racing along the bank. Luckily, I was wearing my straw hat and there were more wasps on its brim than my face. I swiped them and batted them, but several found the back of my neck and hands and zapped me. I tore them off, jumping about like a fish out of water, until Roy came along and somehow brushed the remaining insects away.

I would live to cast again, even though my hands were swollen and throbbing, even though I had a pain in the neck.

Mick's barbel was a glorious-looking specimen, well over eight pounds. I like to think, however, he was even more impressed with the netting than the fish. And luckily he said he had the world's most effective antidote for wasp stings. He simply pointed into the river and told me to get my rod and cast a bait there.

The barbel were obviously in a fine hunger that evening. Within five minutes of casting, the rod was jagged powerfully over. A fish dived into the weeds, was forced out again and then went ballistic on the surface. I was glad it never once made a serious bid for the tail of the pool. He kept more or less to the same area of river and we netted him without any further drama.

It was another beautiful eight pounder and, as Mick had said, it had an instant effect on the wasp stings. Suddenly I didn't notice them at all.

CHAPTER 15

Radio Days

Given the choice, I think I would always go for radio rather than television when making fishing programmes. Television may be more colourful, but radio can be even more atmospheric. It can be tremendously exciting when the camera gets really involved in the drama and beauty of its subject. But radio has the advantage of more effectively feeding the imagination while television is more a feast for the eyes alone.

The main reason radio is superior to TV, however, is that there are almost no restrictions involved. It's just you and the microphone, while television demands constant attention to light, position, camera angle, movement, continuity, composition etc. If you want the fish and the fisherman to behave naturally, you want as few limitations and as little disturbance as possible. When I worked onthe TV series *A Passion for Angling* there was only a one-man camera crew (Hugh Miles) but usually there are at least three involved in television and sometimes as many as 12, including technicians.

With radio, an angler could go solo, though it usually works better when there is an interviewer to keep the dialogue rolling. Obviously, it's an advantage if he is an angler himself, though if he's really keen there's a danger he could take charge of the fishing as well as the commentary - as I discovered last season, to my cost. The cost of a pair of trousers.

Nick Fisher wanted to do a carp angling programme with me for BBC Radio 5 Live's *Dirty Tackle,* a regular slot on Saturday mornings. He didn't necessarily want me to catch him a big fish or *any* fish, he just hoped we could evoke the spirit of classic carping for the microphone. 'No problem,' I assured him.

We got down to the chosen lake at about 3pm, a civilised time to go fishing, especially if you've enjoyed a good lunch. Conditions were perfect – a warm gusty breeze after a wet morning, flashes of sunshine and best of all, no one else fishing.

Nick and I sat down under a line of bankside trees and with the recorder going we talked about the character of the lake and the peculiarities of the carp. Then a lovely great mirror sailed into view only 20 feet away and delved into the silt for bloodworm. Up to the surface rose a flowering of bubbles. My heart rose too, for it was rare to discover those particular carp feeding in the middle of the day and if you did find one feeding, there was a good chance of catching it. I sprinkled a few maggots near the bubble cloud and then followed up with a freelined hook of grubs, ten maggots on a size 8 eyed. Nick whispered his description of events into the microphone, while I tensely waited for the line to twitch. But the carp wasn't tempted to join us and he drifted off after five minutes.

I was pleased that Nick mentioned I was using one of Richard Walker's old MK IVs but I shouldn't have revealed the presence of another such rod in my holdall. I might have guessed what would happen. Within minutes there were two MK IVs fishing side by side, Nick having tackled up the spare faster than I could say 'but'. The carp didn't return to the first chosen pitch, so we crept along the bank until we found a second bubbler frothing even more enthusiastically than the first. With just a single swan shot on the line to add the required distance, Nick dropped his maggots to the right of the bubbles, while I went to the left. Then we waited to see in which direction he'd turn.

As we waited, we quietly talked about the improving prospects and the quality of the weather and then something interrupted the commentary. Nick Fisher, seasoned interviewer, star of screen and radio, dropped his recorder into the bankside undergrowth and dived onto his rod. All thoughts of professional programme making were forgotten as his line tightened, he struck and a whomphing bow wave cleaved across the lake.

There were 100 yards of 9lb line on the old Ambidex reel and by the end of the carp's first rush, Nick only had about ten yards left. As he tried to re-gain some control, I remembered the point of our exercise and rescued the recorder from the brambles. I was obviously surplus to angling requirements, so we swapped roles. I took over the microphone while Nick wrestled with a monster. From the breathless, incomprehensible splutterings on the tape, a listener could have been forgiven for thinking the situation had got a little out of hand.

'Don't let him run to the left or you've had it!'

'I can't hold him!'

'Get the rod point under the water, keep the line out of the overhanging branch.'

'I can't, I've got the rod point stuck in the branch over my head!'

The carp swept imperiously round this huge overhanging alder bough and because he couldn't get the angle of the rod low enough, Nick's line soon became wondrously meshed in the clutching twigs and leaves. The excitement that had risen to fever pitch gradually calmed with the realisation that the fish was well and truly stuck. And worse, with half the branch in the water and a barbless hook, there was a strong possibility that we'd seen the last of it. Pity, as it looked a good twenty-pounder. Suddenly, there was a big boiling splash and the branch shook. The line squealed and creaked but didn't break and miraculously the carp remained attached. I hung the recorder round Nick's neck, as he hung onto the still throbbing rod. Then, as he described the unfolding crisis, I grabbed the net and waded out into three foot of water and three foot of soft glutinous mud. Just as well there wasn't five inches more or I'd have needed a snorkel!

As I slowly worked myself through the depths, the sun burst out and in its light I could clearly see a big mirror carp tethered to the branch. There was no question of disentangling it, but as the fish thrust down I was able to grab hold of the last yard of line and actually lead the carp over the net. It was in the mesh before it knew what had happened. With a final splash and a shout of triumph, I burst out from under the leaves and waded towards Nick who was exclaiming joyfully into the microphone. He became even more euphoric when I lifted the net clear of the water and he saw exactly what we'd got. A superb, linear mirror. It pulled the balance to 25lb 8oz.

We photographed and released it and squelched contentedly back towards home for tea - at least I squelched! All the elements of carp fishing had been captured on tape: the tranquillity, the expectancy, the drama, the crisis and finally the carp itself. It was a pity, though, that we couldn't also convey the authentic smell of vintage black mud so familiar to anyone who's waded into a carp pond. But not even television could manage that.

CHAPTER 16

Crossed Lines

Inspired by Nick Fisher's carp I went back to the lake a few days after we'd made the programme. The conditions had remained the same, the carp would probably still be feeding and I wanted to fish the same pitch as before - and do it without leaping in this time.

It was about 10am when I reached the pool. A fellow carp-head, Bob Davies, was fishing halfway up the east bank and he'd brought a guest, Paul, who was fishing the shallows. The Radio Pitch, down near the dam, was unoccupied and as I crept into it I saw, much to my delight, that a fish was truffling on the lake bed just beyond the leaning alder.

I quickly set up a rod, tied a size 8 hook to the line

and pinched on a swan shot. Then I baited with half a dozen maggots and put a cast as gently as I could next to the disturbance.

Within a few minutes the line peeled off the reel. I struck and in came a sparkling common carp of about two pounds.

Maybe his grandfather would be along later. I baited the area twenty yards out with a pint of maggots and, instead of continuing with a solitary bait, I set up a second rod, casting one to the left and one to the right. It was a comfortable pitch to fish, especially on that tranquil autumn day. Two hours went peacefully by and I was just about to drain my flask when a tremendous burst of bubbles rose over the left-hand bait. I was going to drop my tea mug, but the bubbles gradually fizzled out. I remained motionless, however, not able to raise the mug to my lips again. Suddenly the line poured through the rod rings. I jettisoned the tea and dived forward, but as I went to grab the rod, I somehow caught the line from the other one round my right forefinger. I didn't realise this until I'd turned the reel handle and struck, cleverly looping two lengths of line onto one reel.

Out in the lake there was a great upswirl of water followed by a colossal splash. The rod - a genuine Walker Mark Four Carp - went into a critical bend and the one line from the rod tip zinged towards its breaking point. It was a horrible sensation, but the renegade line had so tangled round my reel that I could neither give nor retrieve an inch.

Incredibly, nothing broke and instead of charging

out into the pool, the carp swept across to my left, surprising me by its turn of speed and not giving me time to get the rod tip under the surface. The eight pound line cut into the alder branch and, just as before, got hopelessly snagged amongst the leaves and seed pods.

There was another big kersplash and the whole tree seemed to shake, but the branch acted like a shock absorber. Even so, I was amazed that the line - and the hook hold - stood the test. I leaned out as far as possible and felt everything creaking as the carp took all the extra yards I could give it.

The untidy spiral of lines down by the reel made a depressing sight and no matter how I tweaked and jagged, I couldn't untangle them. I was even more stuck than Nick had been, especially as I had no-one to gillie for me. There was only one option, and as the carp continued to wallow dangerously under the boughs, I feverishly cut into the tangle with a pair of scissors, praying I wouldn't snip through the wrong line. After five or six almost random cuts, everything pulled miraculously clear and I was in proper contact for the first time. I let the fish take a few feet, but he seemed almost reluctant to leave his sanctuary for open water, nor could I free the line from the branch, no matter how much it see-sawed back and forth through the leaves.

I whistled for assistance and in a minute Bob and Paul were with me, sizing up my predicament. Bob swung out into the tree, taking the landing net with him, but he couldn't reach the fish, though he could see it, now lying quite still beneath the surface.

'It's a mirror,' he said. 'Quite a good one.'

'There's only one thing I can do,' I said. I gave Paul my rod and told him to keep the pressure steady and to give line if the carp panicked. Taking the net, I plunged once more into the lake and followed my still-visible footprints through the deep silt. The carp obviously didn't suspect me as I reached forward throught the screen of leaves and before it realised what was happening it found itself gently cradled in mesh.

I drew it towards me and peered down between the net arms. It was, as Bob had said, a good fish, but it wasn't a mirror after all. I unhooked it in the water and brought it ashore where it weighed in at $27\frac{3}{4}$ pounds. It was a common carp and probably the most exquisitely scaled specimen I had ever seen. But it was also the daftest I'd ever hooked. It had everything going for it, I did everything wrong, yet somehow it still ended up on the bank.

If Nick had been there to make a second episode for radio his listeners would never have believed it.

CHAPTER 17

Tea and Mystery

This is a mystery that almost every angler will be familiar with. You have been fishing for several hours without a bite and, desiring refreshment and inspiration, you feel the time has come for a tea break. Before opening your flask you do one of two things, you either reel in and lay the rod to one side or, if your method permits it, simply leave the rod in the rest and forget about it. As you pour the scalding liquid into your teacup so the spell is cast.

For all those hours you were assiduously fishing nothing had stirred in the dark depths before you. Indeed, all the fish in the river were very carefully avoiding you and your bait. However, as soon as the tea starts to fill your cup every roach, chub, barbel, perch, bream, dace, gudgeon, pike, carp, grayling, loach and bullhead in the vicinity begins to feed voraciously. Naturally, if you didn't reel in, your bait is grabbed by the nearest specimen, but because you have both hands occupied the result is inevitably tragic. Out of the corner of your eye you see either the float zip under or the rod tip pull round and, in a desperate attempt to strike, you spill boiling hot tea in your lap. The consequent pain causes you to leap high into the air, kicking the rod from the rest in the process. The flask is broken, the tea cup empty and, of course, the strike is missed. Moreover, the unholy commotion terrifies the fish and they stop feeding for the rest of the day.

This mystery is only made stranger when you consider what would have happened if you'd reeled in before opening your flask. The fish would still have started feeding the moment you poured the tea, but, apart from an occasional rise on the surface, you probably wouldn't have been aware of what was happening. You innocently sip your refreshing beverage, enjoying every mouthful, and you might even pour yourself a second cup. Unseen by you, the fish continue their ravenous feeding binge which only ends when, magically, they realise you are screwing the cup back on the empty flask. With hope restored after your welcome break, you cast once more, but your optimism is unfounded and you end the day with another blank. Because this phenomenon is so familiar, anglers have, over the years, tried to take advantage of it, cunningly opening their flasks with one hand, while holding the rod with the other. But of course fish are not stupid. They will never bite in these circumstances – they wait until the angler has given up hope; they wait until he is draining the last mouthful, tipping his head back and tilting the magic tea cup so that he can't see that his float is suddenly being pulled under or the rod almost pulled out of the rest.

But now I think I might have stumbled on a way to make the magic work positively. I was fishing the flooded Hampshire Avon last January, hoping for a barbel or chub in the quieter slacks and eddies. I hadn't had a bite for two hours. Then I spotted my comrade-in-rods, Demus Canning, and went over to have a chat with him. He hadn't had a bite all day either, despite his best efforts.

'Have a cup of tea,' I said, taking my flask from my creel. 'Thank you,' said Demus.'Have a cast into my swim.'

So while Demus poured the tea I fished his swim and the inevitable happened. Before he'd even filled the cup a 4lb chub grabbed my bait. Needless to say, it was the only fish – in fact the only bite – of the day. I didn't consider this important at the time, but the next time I went fishing further downstream on the Avon the same thing happened again. I'd been fishing a quiet glide out of the main flow, but there'd been no response to my careful searching of the swim with a rolling leger. Then a friend appeared, also complaining of lack of fish.

'Nevermind,' I said. 'Have a cup of tea.' I passed him my flask and as he was pouring so the fish reacted in the usual way, except, as before, I was ready for them. The rod tip banged over, the centrepin squealed and a 6lb barbel took off powerfully down the main current. Very interesting, I thought, as I eventually slipped the net under the golden beauty. Of course there were no more chances in that spot, so I moved swims, deliberately choosing a stretch that didn't look terribly inviting where the speed of the flood water meant I had to use a heavy leger to hold bottom. There were several other anglers about, though hardly any of them had caught anything and I knew one of them would eventually pass me by, looking for a more promising swim. When this finally happened – after another biteless hour – I surprised the unknown fisher person by inviting him to have a cup of tea. And it worked! I jest not! Another barbel – 7lb this time.

The conditions were perfect during the last week of the season and lots of big fish were taken, whether the anglers concerned were drinking tea or not. Spring arrived early, the banks of the Avon were gilded with celandine and primrose and the birds began their familiar songs. I went down to the Royalty with Shaun Linsley and I felt our optimism was justified, the air temperature was in the mid-50s and the water temperature 49° Fahrenheit and rising. Furthermore, the sky was overcast, the breeze gentle and the river was at normal level for the first time this year. When we discovered, to our delight, that our favoured swims were unoccupied, it seemed certain we'd get a fish first cast, yet the minutes passed and there was no tremor of response from the barbel. After two hours without a bite I suddenly remembered the new trick and invited Shaun to come upstream and have a cup of tea. I actually laid my rod down on the bank (with the bait still in the water, of course) as I took the flask out of my creel. I passed it to Shaun saying 'This will guarantee a fish!' Shaun just laughed, but he remembers my words and what happened afterwards. He is my witness (though he might be reluctant to admit it). He poured the tea and my rod tip, which had been slightly curved, suddenly straightened as a fish picked up the bait and came downstream with it. I snatched up the rod from the grass, struck and there was a barbel – a big one, too. It kept deep, nosing slowly and powerfully upstream against all the strain of the rod and the force of the current. But I got him in the end, my best barbel of the season, just over 11lb.

The drawback with this new method, however, is that while I may be catching more fish, I hardly ever get a cup of tea.

CHAPTER 18

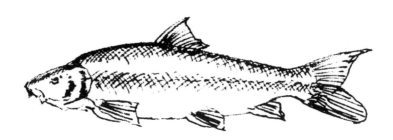

Switching off

It happened again today. That makes eight times in total these last few seasons. Eight rather strange angling incidents which have now convinced me there is a definite advantage in switching off.

For about three hours I'd been fishing a nice day ticket stretch of the Hampshire Avon. The weather had improved recently and very pleasant it was to sit amongst the willow herb on a warm autumn afternoon watching the last swallows flying southwards and hoping for a barbel to snatch my bait. The weather may have improved, but the dreams of William, my seven-year-old, have gone dark these last nights and my sleep, therefore, has suffered in consequence. But now, with the river sliding by almost hypnotically, and the fish not in evidence, I could happily catch up on a little unfinished business. I put the rod in the rest, switched on the reel check, pulled my hat over my eyes, lay

101

back and drifted contentedly into oblivion.

Perhaps half an hour passed. Suddenly I woke up, completely alert and focused. Nothing had changed. The river flowed along the same as before, the rod was in the same position with the line quivering gently in the current. But I was convinced something was going to happen. I reeled in, rebaited with a little sliver of luncheon meat on a size 8 hook, recast and waited expectantly. A few moments passed and then the rod tip went tick tick tock and I was into a powerful muscular barbel that, when I eventually landed it, weighed just a whisker under 9lb. It was the only fish of the day. Though I managed to get my baits onto the noses of several others, there were no more takers.

In itself, this hardly seems worthy of mention, but there have been many such incidents. For example, last season I was fishing that same bit of river but in a different swim. I'd spoken to a few other anglers on my walk downstream and they'd all complained of straight rods. Not a fish had been caught, though by then it was mid-afternoon. I plonked myself down at a promising looking swim and began fishing with corn. After an hour, I saw a good barbel shadow across the gravel between two plumes of weed – so at least I knew I was in the right place. Then I saw three smaller specimens browsing over the river bed. Yet though I fished quite intensely the bait was not even nudged. Eventually, I put the rod in a rest and poured myself a cup of tea from the flask. Every angler knows the dangers and benefits of pouring tea when fishing. But though I was convinced something would happen, it didn't. That almost persuaded me to go home early. However, the tea tasted good, and relishing the last heat of the sinking sun, I made myself comfortable on the grassy bank and enjoyed a doze. As happened today, I woke abruptly, feeling very sharp and keen, and not in the least groggy. Usually, I feel like I've got a mild hangover when I wake from a daytime nap (not that I often get a chance nowadays for such a luxury).

The sun had sunk out of sight behind the willows on the far bank, but everything else was unchanged and, as before, the rod had not moved. I watched it intently for about five minutes, sensing that I should not reel in and rebait, but simply wait for the inevitable.

Wham! The rod almost leapt out of the rest and the reel was howling before I could get my hands on it. A 7lb barbel eventually rolled into the net, the only one to be taken on the fishery that day. The same kind of thing has happened numerous times though not always in the same way, or just when I've been after barbel. Chub, tench and carp have all responded to my switching off.

Of course, this kind of phenomenon has not been unnoticed by other anglers. I remember reading an article by one of Redmire's first fishermen, the late Dick Kefford, in which he wrote of the advantages of lessening your concentration when you were fishing for big carp. His advice was to read a book and this is something I used to do anyway, especially when I was on a week's stint at Redmire. For example, I recall an occasion back in 1973 when I became engrossed in that epic story about talking rabbits, *Watership Down*. Then, suddenly, I got to a line that I couldn't finish. It was a highly charged dramatic moment in the book, yet there was an even more highly charged moment in the air. If I'd been asleep, it would have woken me up and yet, perhaps, if I'd been actively doing something, if I hadn't mentally switched off, then maybe I wouldn't have noticed it.

I put the book down and looked across the pool. Nothing was happening, and yet everything was happening. I waited for only a few seconds, then picked up my rod and hurried down to the dam, about a hundred yards distant. Right in the dam corner, just where the water shelved into the deeps, there was a big cluster of bubbles. I baited a size 6 hook with a red kidney bean and just lowered it into the bubble cloud. I was using a quill float and after a while it slid slowly and purposefully away. Something headed across the pool, making my centrepin grizzle. My old angling chum, Rod Hutchinson, came leaping over a stile. He thought I'd hooked Redmire's monster gudgeon, but it was even bigger than that; a mirror of 38lb.

Exactly a year ago as I write, it was the 44th anniversary of Richard Walker's famous 44lb carp, caught at Redmire in 1952. Having a great affection for Walker and the story of that great fish, a few friends and I always like to celebrate the day he caught it by going carp fishing somewhere. Last year, I arranged to meet two angling friends, John Ginifer and Mick Canning, at a favourite local water and such was my enthusiasm, I even got there first – something that never happens normally.

The lake was deserted, the sky was blue, the morning sun was just above the woods; a perfect September day. Furthermore, the carp were bubbling well and a few pouches of maggots got them going even more fervently. By the time Mick and John arrived it was nearly three hours since I had first cast and I'd not had a single take. My line hadn't even quivered and I was almost getting despondent.

The two anglers strode along the bank to greet me and I produced a flask of rather fine whisky so that we could make a toast in remembrance of an historic angling event. I was standing now a few yards behind my rod. We raised our glasses and said: 'To Richard Walker and his great fish.' At that precise moment the silver foil indicator on my line whipped up to the butt ring and the line went hissing through it. Amid much merry banter and laughter, a beautiful looking 9lb common carp came walloping over the net.

We all settled down to fish but though there was plenty of bubbling over the groundbait we waited by our rods for more than an hour without any response. 'Time for a cup of tea,' I announced and fired up my Kelly Kettle. I'd

105

had my back to the lake for about two minutes and then whoosh! the line gushed off the open spool and the result was another splendid common.

I had two more carp that day and both picked up the bait the moment I'd turned away from the lake with something other than fishing on my mind. There have been scores of other similar episodes that point either to an unbelievably regular series of mere coincidences or something rather more interesting.

These are just examples of switching off but there are countless other ways of turning attention away from the fish. Sometimes, as I said earlier, the advantages of switching off are not related to the hypersensitivity of the fish but to your own awareness.

By switching off you reduce your mental activity and yet become actually more aware of what is going on. All those daft little thoughts that were pecking away at your consciousness are simply forgotten and, by winding down, you discover a greater appreciation of your surroundings. Then sometimes It may happen that you feel something that you can't logically understand and yet, because you are a fisherman, you react instinctively and sometimes catch a fish you would otherwise have missed.

But I believe that it's just as important to remember how incredibly aware the fish are of the angler. Naturally, if the fish are already feeding confidently or are, in other respects, relaxed or preoccupied then I can be as concentrated or sometimes even as visible as I like. It won't affect them. Or I can induce them to feed confidently by careful and patient groundbaiting. Yet often there is nothing I can do, especially if I am after a big, wily old specimen. He's not going to play because even if he can't see me he can feel me. Fish can 'see' through their skins and I'm convinced that, for most of the time I'm fishing for him, a wild fish is somehow conscious of my presence. He may be feeding but the realisation that I am hanging about with intent will make him very difficult to catch. However, if he thinks I have lost interest in him, then he might well pick up my bait.

CHAPTER 19

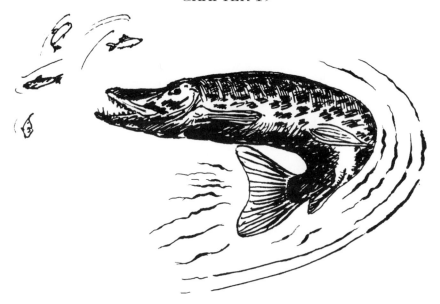

The Unexpected Pike

We arrived at the river just after sunrise and, as usual, the three of us – David, Will and myself (all aged 12 at the time) – peered over the bridge before we began fishing. It was the customary thing to do; firstly, we liked to have a proper look at the river and, secondly, we liked to watch the little fish playing in the clear water beneath the arch. Usually, we could see minnows and small dace, but, if we were lucky, we might sometimes spot a chub or a roach or a perch. On the day in question, however, we saw none of these. We all craned over the parapet and gasped at the sight of a monstrous pike. We had never seen such a huge fish before. Naturally, we had seen other pike, but none that looked even half the size of that lunker. He just lay quietly below us in midstream, his great pectorals working gently, his gill plates slowly pulsing, his tail barely quivering.

The water was clear and not particularly deep so we could see every pale stripe along his back and, more excitingly, we caught the movement of the eyes when they appeared to swivel upwards and stare directly at us. It was enough to turn a boy to stone.

I remember thinking that, however impressive it looked, there was absolutely no point in fishing for such a leviathan. What chance could we have of landing it? We all had fine-tipped cane roach rods and centrepins loaded with about 20 yards of 4lb line. Moreover, I had no desire to grapple with such a diabolical looking creature. The more I stared at it the more convinced I became that, had I fallen in, it would have swallowed me whole. Will seemed to share my opinion, but David had no such qualms.

'Right then,' he said, 'if you two can catch me a gudgeon or a dace, I'll catch the pike.'

'Why can't you fish for gudgeon as well?' I asked.

'I'm going home, dopey! I'll grab my dad's sea-fishing gear and be back here in an hour.'

He raced off up the lane on his bike and Will and I were left on the bridge, still staring down at the pike.

'Even if he hooks it, how are we going to land it?' said Will, echoing my own doubts. We had not reached that happy stage in our angling careers when landing nets were a necessity. On those rare occasions when we connected with something astonishing, like a half-pound roach, we could usually manage to swing it safely ashore or lift it out by hand. But even if we had owned a landing net it certainly wouldn't have been large enough for a monster pike.

However, we didn't believe David would actually persuade the pike to take a bait, not unless he used a sheep, therefore the problem of landing it would not arise. We went downstream to a favourite spot – a deep eddy under a leaning oak – and, as usual, fished for whatever came along. It seemed that only about 10 minutes had passed when we saw David hurrying down the bank towards us, carrying a bundle of old sea-fishing tackle. He looked not only exhausted but also dismayed. Perhaps he'd guessed that we hadn't yet caught him a fish. 'What's up?' I asked.

'It's gone!' he said. 'I just looked over the bridge and there's no sign of it. You didn't frighten it off, did you, or cast a worm at it?'

We put down our rods and went back upstream to see for ourselves. Sure enough, the monster had vanished and the usual tiddlers had returned to their familiar playground under the arch. We scouted about a bit, looking into all the likely fish-holding spots up and downstream, but we could not find it.

'What a waste of a chance!' whined David. 'If only I'd had some stronger line on me when we first arrived.'

We went back to the oak tree pool and had an enjoyable morning catching dace and little roach. Then Will had a bite on a worm and pulled out a superb gudgeon that must have been seven inches long. David hooked a chub that must have taken two yards of line from the reel before he beached it. Then I had a genuine six-inch roach. By sandwich time we had almost forgotten about the pike but, after guzzling a bottle of Tizer, David sneaked back up to the bridge. He was only gone a couple of minutes, then he came quietly back, resigned to the fact that he'd probably never see the giant again. Sometime during the middle of the afternoon my yellow-tipped quill bobbed once, twice, then zipped away sideways and I hooked a good fish.

'Hey!' I shouted. 'This is a big one.'

I'd been using the tail of a lob and it had been taken by a perch. We caught a glimpse of it after a few moments, the fins all bristling and the black stripes looking tigerish in the deep water.

'Whoa!' said David, 'That must be over a pound.'

My rod curved superbly and we watched the way the line cut out across the river. It swung out to about midstream, then began swinging back towards us. Suddenly, there was a terrific wave shooting upstream, as if an invisible speedboat had swept past taking the perch with it.

Of course, it was the big pike. At first I was

112

shocked, even terrified, but then I was simply angry. It was such a foul trick! My lovely perch snatched away by a great snaggle-toothed pike. After a minute though, the pressure eased, the rod came back into a more manageable bend and I reeled in my prize fish. Amazingly, there was hardly a scratch on it and we rejoiced over one of the biggest perch we'd ever seen. It weighed $1\frac{1}{4}$ lb on our rusty old spring balance.

David did not spend long admiring it, however. Within a few minutes he had set up his dad's old boat rod and a wooden star-back reel, hooked a dead dace onto some kind of shark hook and cast out into mid stream. The dace sank slowly to the bottom and the thick, tightly coiled line gradually straightened in the gentle current. We expected an instant take and yet when it came, after only a few minutes, we all jumped. The line twitched once then cut away downstream under the overhanging boughs of the oak. Waiting just a few seconds, David struck and the broom-handle of a rod went into a partial bend. He'd hooked it! It seemed incredible, impossible; it also seemed dangerous. There was a powerful dragging force that almost pulled David into the river. We pleaded with him to let the fish have line, but he was determined to simply hang on.

'I'm not giving it an inch,' he gasped. But he had to in the end or he really would have gone in. However, the pike must have realised the tackle was virtually unbreakable, even though David was not using a wire trace. After

113

that initial, ferocious lunge, it merely went round and round, deep down, for about three minutes, and then David began reeling it in. We all gawped as we watched it materialise from the depths. First we saw the great shovel of a head then the staring eyes followed by the looming length of its crocodile body. Under the bank, it lay quite still and for a moment we all stood staring down at it, wondering what to do. We certainly weren't going to attempt to lift it ashore in our arms and David obviously could not heave it bodily out of the water. But a few yards downstream there was a place where a dried up ditch entered the river and after juggling the rod round the oak trunk, David worked the fish along the bank and without any help from us, managed to beach it, or rather, ditch it.

On the bank it looked almost more impressive than it had done under the bridge. A huge-looking, beautifully marked fish that seemed almost as long as me. Out of his element, though, it had lost its malevolence. We could touch it without fear. Of course, we couldn't weigh it properly. It must have been around 15lb, but our spring balance could not cope with anything so spectacular. And our 12-inch 'Fisherman's Ruler' looked absurd next to it. Luckily, the shank of the hook was protruding from the forest of teeth, though the unhooking still had the crisis atmosphere of a bomb disposal exercise.

'Are you going to take it home?' I asked.

'It would look great strapped to your crossbar!'

said Will.

'No,' said David. 'If I took it home my dad would never believe I'd caught it on my tackle, so he'd know that I'd taken his stuff – without asking. He'd never have lent it to me, no matter how nicely I'd asked.'

'What!' I said. 'Surely he's not worried about you breaking it?'

'You don't know my dad!'

But we would probably have put the pike back anyway. We had had the adventure, the drama; David had had the glory; the monster had had his come-uppance.

Together, we carefully lifted it up and half lowered it, half rolled it back into the river. For a moment it lay on its side like a capsized tanker. Only gradually did it seem to rediscover itself: first a pectoral wagged, then the tail began to sway, pushing it, still sideways, upstream for a yard or two. Then, lazily, it righted itself, hung a moment near the surface and finally sank down into the deeps, its menace returning as it faded from sight.

'Let's see if we can catch another perch,' said Will. 'Or another chub,' I said. 'You carry on,' said David. 'I've got to get this old gear back before my dad gets home from work. See you tomorrow.' But he was back with his own rod within the hour.

CHAPTER 20

The Unexpected Chub

A friend of mine, Mem 'Jardine' Hassan, had a ticket on a stretch of the Hampshire Avon that was only ever fished by salmon anglers. Jardine was keen to catch an Avon salmon, but the days of the big spring fish were over and the only real opportunities lay in the summer, when the grilse were running. This, of course, meant that he often packed a barbel or chub rod when he went salmon fishing; for while he was searching for the 'silver tourists', he would often stumble on a shoal of 'natives'. And one July day he stumbled on a fish so big that he thought his eyes must be deceiving him. But he wasn't seeing things. I'm certain of that because I was his guest that day and I saw the monster too.

We had been half-heartedly looking for a salmon during the early morning, but there wasn't a sign of even a small grilse in all the usual holding pools. There was a wide stretch of shallows that ran suddenly into a deeper, narrower glide and we knew from previous experience that a shoal of barbel would be waiting for us there. So we put away our salmon gear, tackled up our proper rods and sneaked into position through the willow herb. We began feeding maggots into the swim and Jardine peered through the cover to see if we were attracting anything. I tossed in another handful upstream of him and as the maggots sank something emerged from the weed beds.

'Blimming heck!' gasped Jardine, and he turned to me with his jaw dropped and his eyes boggled.

'What is it?' I whispered, not being able to see clearly through the undergrowth. Jardine crawled out of the hole he'd made in the willow herb and said: 'Have a look yourself. You won't believe it!' He looked stunned.

I inched forward until I had a clear view into the swim, put on my polarising glasses, blinked and said: 'It must be a carp! No, it looks like a bass! No, it's a clonking great chub!'

Now I have seen a couple of very big chub before, even if the biggest I've caught was only 5lb 12oz. I reckon, in the distant past, that I might have seen an eight-pounder, but this Avon fish was much, much bigger. Both

Jardine and I reckon it must have been almost 30 inches long and would have weighed 10lb easily. It was definitely picking off one or two maggots as they drifted past it and we got a clearer idea of its dimensions when it was suddenly joined by several barbel that looked in the 6lb to 7lb category. The chub dwarfed them all! Unlike the graceful quick-finned barbel, the monster seemed cumbersome, even awkward in its movements. It looked an ancient specimen and the large scales had a rough-edged, slightly irregular appearance. It dropped lower in the water, as if dragged down by its great weight.

We both crawled away out of sight and Jardine feverishly set up float tackle while I tossed in a few more maggots. Then he cast from a few yards upstream and we honestly thought he was going to hook the chub straight away. It was such an unexpected surprise, in such an accessible spot, that it surely meant our luck was in and we were destined to break the record.

But, of course, Jardine didn't hook the chub. The first fish he caught was one of the barbel, a six-pounder that seemed awfully small compared to the giant. He graciously let me have a cast and a bit of trundled luncheon meat produced an instant lunging take.

'Is it him?' asked Jardine.

'No,' I said, seeing the streamlined form of a barbel spearing itself into the weed. It was the one we thought had weighed about 7lb and we were, after a bit of a tussle, proved almost right: 6lb 14oz. Naturally, after that the chub disappeared and we didn't see it again. But we guessed it hadn't gone far into the dense weedbeds and continued fishing, hopefully, for the rest of the day.

The barbel were in an eager frame of mind and we caught seven by sunset on maggots, meat and sweetcorn. Every time one of the rods bent into a fish our hearts skipped a few beats with the thought that, this time, it might be super-chub; but it never was.

However, just as the light was fading in the west, I hooked a big fish after dropping a bait right across the river into a narrow gap in the weeds. It ploughed off downstream and eventually came to an unbudgeable stop. I tried every trick in the book to shift it, but finally the hook sprang free.

It just might have been.....

CHAPTER 21

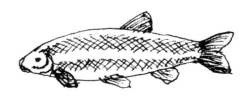

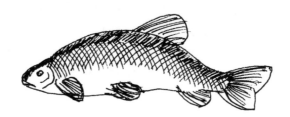

A High Standard Cast

Henry told me about a very big chub he'd stumbled upon at a place on the river Rother below Fittleworth. We had caught many good fish from that stretch during the preceding years, though only one of them went over the coveted five-pound mark. Now Henry had seen a monster lying up in the shadow of a dense overhanging alder. He described the spot precisely and said the chub was definitely 'over the six', so naturally I went down to have a peek.

There is a kind of understanding between angling friends which says that if someone discovers an especially large fish then he has the divine right to cast first and even to forbid anyone else near it until he either catches it or gives up in the attempt. Friends being friends, however, there is also a second kind of understanding that acknowledges how a big fish can sometimes cause a remarkably easy break in the bonds of loyalty. But Henry had assured me there was no chance of him or anyone else getting anywhere near the old chub as it lay in such an inaccessible nest of alder branches. He had not even attempted a cast, which therefore enabled me to approach the monster's sanctuary with a fairly clear conscience, even though I was carrying a rod.

It was below a pool on a bend which we called The Forest, owing to the arboreal aspect, a place of surprisingly deep water where, particularly in winter, there was nearly always a chance for a fish or two. The river swept round and then down along an avenue of alders. The second and third trees lowered several big branches actually into the water and amongst these the chub spent his dappled days.

I crawled up to the edge of the bank through tall hogweed and nettles, then peered down between the leaves and twigs, letting my eyes grow accustomed to the sudden darkness, hoping that eventually I'd be able to tell the difference between a shadow or reflection and a fish. It didn't take long. A dark smudge seemed to become darker and more obviously fish shaped. Chub shaped. Then it became more smudgy again, its vastness skewing my focus. It was probably nearer seven than six.

Chuckling, I lowered my head slowly and crawled backwards into the open field. It was going to be tricky, but it certainly wasn't as impossible as Henry had led me to believe, though maybe this was because the chub had moved out of the densest area of forest. I had an ideal rod for the task: a seven-foot Hardy Wanless No.2 (for 6lb line). It was slightly overloaded, as I'd coupled it to an Aerial and

8lb line, but I knew it was steely enough to take the extra strain. Having tackled up, I slid the net into position, then, with a matchbox size piece of crust, I squirmed back to the edge of the bank and waited five minutes before attempting a cast. It would have been fatal to try anything before ensuring that (a) the chub was oblivious of me and (b) I knew exactly where to place the bait. What happened if I connected would depend more on luck than skill, which suited my style. The fish hung a few inches below the surface, with a biggish branch spreading out its foliage between him and me. However, by swinging an underhand cast upstream I could probably get the crust to drift down beneath the leaves and then stab the rod into the river if the chub took it. Many other branches swooped down across the water upstream and also behind me and around me so the cast would have to be as accurate as I could make it - which again left luck to do most of the work. Yet, after gently swinging the bait like a pendulum for a tick-tock-tick-tock, I flicked it forward on the next 'tick' and braked the reel almost as soon as it began to spin, bringing the crust down quickly but gently just short of the foliage. It hardly made a ripple as it landed in the narrow two-foot wide channel between bank and branches.

The current brought it slowly back towards me, just far enough out for its course to take it almost directly over the waiting chub. But then the line from the rod tip caught on a little pesky twig. I couldn't free it and the crust began to drag on the surface.

Damn it! If only I'd kept the rod point down at

water level as I'd told myself. I had to flick the hook free and let the bread carry on without me to the spot where it was quietly and confidently engulfed by a huge pair of white lips.

But the chub didn't submerge and disappear; he remained on station, waiting to see what else the current would bring him. The second cast was a bit riskier than the first as I made it without any preparatory swing, impatient to get a bait in the water again. It was perfect, though, and this time I made sure the rod tip stayed low. Yet it wasn't quite perfect - it was drifting downstream slightly further out than before.

As it floated along, the bait was only partially visible. I could see it only when it passed under small breaks in the overhanging branches, but just when I was expecting it to reappear in one of these, I heard a rippling and the line suddenly cut up through the surface.

Out of the corner of my eye I could still see the motionless shadow of the big chub. Something else was down there.

I struck and plunged the rod tip underwater. Two big splashes erupted simultaneously - one from the hooked fish, one from the monster. The rod kicked and shook, but I didn't have to give line and soon managed to steer a very unwelcome three-pounder into the net.

The monster didn't reappear and I never saw it again. More unfortunately, neither did Henry.

CHAPTER 22

The Almost Perfect Cast

I was at the top of the lookout tree on one of Redmire's islands, spending a quiet summer afternoon watching the carp as they slowly pushed through vast weedbeds below me. There were numerous fish between ten and twenty pounds, plus a couple that were around the thirty mark, but even these last were made to look very small indeed when a tremendous creature – a mirror – materialised from the weeds only fifteen yards down my island. I recognised it as a fish I'd landed four years previously, when it weighed 38lb. Its distinctive two-tone flank and its pattern of scaling made it unmistakable. But there had been a change since I'd last seen him. He was bigger, not in length but in overall bulk, and I guessed him to weigh well over 40lb. He also looked in much better fettle than before.

As I gazed down on him he actually began to feed,

truffling through the reddish mud for his favourite delicacies. I had a pocket full of beans and I tossed one so that it landed perfectly right in front of the carp's nose. Amazingly, he took it on the drop!

This was too good a chance to miss. It was going to be tricky, but with everything in such clear view from the treetop, it should, I thought, be possible to cast a hook and bait accurately enough. Hooking and playing a big fish in such a precarious position was, I thought going to be fun, though netting might prove problematic.

After sprinkling the area with a few more offerings, I went and got my rod, carefully wove it up through the branches and prepared to cast. The fish was just too far for a freelined bait so I had to add a couple of shot to the line. I flicked out and the beans dropped a couple of yards to the carp's left. Near enough, I thought. He was changing his position as he picked up the loose feed. He was actively searching for it. but then, just as he seemed to be approaching the bait, he turned the wrong way and swam some 20 feet further into the pool.

I reeled up and took aim again wanting this cast to be just a little more precise than before.

Swinging the rod slowly, the tackle flew in a long arc out and down, down, plop! Right on the carp's head.

My polarising glasses had been steaming up because of the tension, but now I couldn't see anything at all because I was laughing. The cast could not have been

126

more perfectly placed to make the fish panic and I didn't see it again for two years.

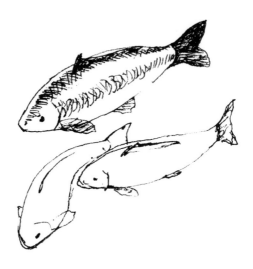

CHAPTER 23

The Great Gudgeon Hunt

The philosophy of the gudgeon fisher is a good one and every angler would be wise to adopt it. Anglers who constantly go in search of what are considered superior quarry, say carp, tench, roach or chub, often return home dejected at the day's end simply because their favourite species didn't want to feed.

But the gudgeon fisher invariably comes home happy because the gudgeon *always* wants to feed. It is such a greedy, silly little fish that it will bite all day long, rain or shine. This fact alone fills the gudgeon angler with so much confidence that, as long as he can find his quarry, he never fails. Therefore, if you always convince yourself that you're fishing for gudgeon, even when you're not, this same wild confidence will grow in you and you'll find it much easier to outwit the specimen you're actually after.

129

The attitude of the gudgeon fisher is a good one, but even better is the attitude of the gudgeon fisher in disguise. This is the secret of my modest success in angling. Whenever I go fishing, I always tell myself that I'm after gudgeon, even if I'm using floating crust on a size 4 hook.

But to work this trick properly, you have to have experienced real gudgeon fishing. In the 19th century, gudgeon scratching, as it was termed, was a hugely popular pastime and whole families would take to the river in punts and spend their summer Sunday afternoons happily catching netsful of speckled silvery fish. Nowadays, the gudgeon is not found in such large shoals any more, but there are still plenty of hot-spots up and down the country and, whenever you discover one, think of it as a gift from old Izaak. Forget your pike and bream, get out your tiddler snatching gear and enjoy yourself.

You need to get into the swing of catching gudgeon, to cast out every time absolutely sure that your float is going to twitch and dart under within seconds. And when you get so blasé that you can catch fish while drinking a cup of tea – without spilling a drop or putting the cup down – then you are a true gudgeon 'scratcher'. At that moment you may cunningly put your tiddler tackle aside, pick up your roach or chub rod and cast with the same absolute confidence for a larger specimen.

Of course it often happens that the larger specimens will succumb to your new powers before you have quite finished your business with the gudgeon. This will probably be all right if it's only a perch or a roach, but certain difficulties may arise if it's a carp or a tench.

I remember various occasions at Redmire when, bored by lack of carp activity, I'd tackle up with a light rod, 3lb line, size 14 hook and floatfish maggots for gudgeon. Redmire gudgeon were once famous for having record breaking potential and it was always a fond hope of mine that I might break both the carp *and* gudgeon records from the same water. But what often happened after I'd got the tiddlers feeding in earnest off the dam was that instead of twitching and bobbing, my float would slide away in an ominously slow and determined manner. My gentle strike would then produce not a record gudgeon but a reel-screeching double-figure carp that might take up to 20 minutes to land. Still, if nothing else, gudgeon fishing at Redmire was an almost guaranteed method of avoiding a carp blank, though I'd often get nervous about having my tiddler snatching so terrifyingly disturbed.

When conditions were good at Redmire, it was actually less exciting to be fishing for carp with the proper gear than angling for gudgeon, for the above reasons. But whenever I was stalking a really large fish I simply had to tell myself 'This is just like gudgeon fishing,' – and the rest would be easy.

As you can imagine, a group of traditionalists like the Golden Scale Club holds the gudgeon in very high esteem. The annual gudgeon party has always been one of the most popular days in the club's calendar. It is, or rather was, often the only day in the season when everybody, even the chairman, caught something. However, over the last few years catches have been well down on previous seasons and a recent outing to the Thames with punts and parasols and greenheart rods produced nothing but chub – a very grave state of affairs. The great gudgeon catches of the past, when dozens of fish would be caught between brew-ups or visits to the village pub, suddenly seemed like an historical fantasy. And of course this meant that it was increasingly difficult to rediscover the true gudgeon fisher's mentality and apply it to other species.

'Where,' asked the club chairman, 'have all the gudgeon gone?'

Well they can't have all just disappeared, like the burbot; maybe they have just altered their habits, or their habitat. And in the meantime, until we discover exactly what's happened to them, we have devised an alternative gudgeon strategy.

This is how it goes. The invitations to the Golden Scale Club. gudgeon party go out as normal in early summer, but the venue is now the Hampshire Avon rather than the Thames or a more famous gudgeon pond. Members are reminded that the Avon gudgeon are a formidable quarry; fine lines and tiny hooks just won't suffice any more. At last season's party there was a fine turnout, with not only regular members, but one or two special guests – tackle merchant Andy Orme and reel maker Richard Carter, with his wife, Sue. We were also delighted by the arrival on the river of our Honorary President, Bernard Venables. Though Avon gudgeon are not caught in the same numbers as ordinary gudgeon, there is a good chance that everyone will at least make contact with a fish, and on last year's trip the conditions for angling were ideal: overcast, still and warm. Yet it was still a couple of hours before the first specimen was hooked. Bernard had missed a good bite and Andy Orme had landed a chub. Mick 'Demus' Canning had just moved into the tail of the pool I was fishing when his rod suddenly curved over. I grabbed my net and ran down the bank as he expertly guided a glorious gudgeon towards him. Then he got another one with his next cast.

The thing about these Avon gudgeon is that they are not silver with blue and purple flecks, but bright gold. Furthermore, they weigh, on average, seventy times more than ordinary gudgeon.

At first glance, there is a strong resemblance to another famous Avon fish, but then gudgeon and barbel do belong to the same family.

CHAPTER 24

Gobio, Oh Gobio!

Nowadays, large angling societies are often run like big businesses, with barbed nosed accountants, merchandising of everything from badges to teapots and society fisheries so carefully organised you get more sense of adventure visiting your auntie.

Compared to this the Golden Scale Club, to which I belong, runs like a donkey on Guinness, but its primary concerns remain constant: to preserve the spirit of angling as well as its traditional values and also to be as enthusiastic about a gudgeon in the rain as a 20lb carp on midsummer morning. However, as fishing is generally a chancy business, the membership has a chancy attitude towards club activities, relying on good fortune and coincidence to decide dates of meetings, the location of an outing or whether or not the chairman should be allowed to catch a fish.

It is all so vague and casual that the entire club can sometimes vanish for a whole year, reappearing suddenly at a favourite pub with all kinds of extravagant plans for the next season.

With such a haphazard approach there is as much potential for disaster as success. And yet the cast falls right more often than not.

Late last year, for instance, a member called Pikeater worked a spell on the river keeper of a wonderful stretch of the Test. Not only did this water occasionally yield 3lb roach, 6lb chub and 4lb grayling, it also contained shoals of fantastic gudgeon. Before the keeper had realised what he was saying, Pikeater got him to invite the members of the Golden Scale Club for a free day's fishing.

The response was very disappointing. Instead of just the usual hard core of four or five accepting the invitation there were 15 enthusiastic takers. Such a dense bristling of split cane would inevitably lead to all kinds of complications, like how many bottles of wine, teapots, cakes and pies to bring and how best to keep other members out of your productive swims. It was a blessing that Hon. President Bernard Venables was going to come. His benign presence always has a marvellous calming effect on the rest of the membership and would therefore ensure only a limited amount of fighting over gudgeon hot spots.

The day in question dawned clear and mild and the anglers converged on the River Test from as far afield as Chester, Cheltenham, Worthing and Dubai. When I finally reached the river I found everyone well established in their chosen swims and some of them even catching fish, though it was still pre-lunchtime. And though the quality of the fishing could not be guaranteed because of heavy overnight rain, at least the quality of the lunch was ensured. The keeper, obviously still under Pikeater's spell, had given us the key to an old and superbly equipped fishing hut, complete with china, cutlery and ten-man kettle.

I leant over a bridge to watch Pikeater trotting for dace and grayling. He was wading well out from the bank, allowing the current to sweep his float under the bridge where, he said, the fish were waiting. Eventually he hooked something that put a terrific bend in his rod. Giant grayling? Specimen chub?

'Hey!' I shouted suddenly. 'Isn't that a carbon rod you're using?'

'No,' replied Pikeater, 'it's charcoal.'

I made a mental note to humiliate him in front of the rest of the club at lunchtime. But then we discovered that the fish was only a silver tourist. So I forgave him but told him he'd only catch real fish if he used a proper rod.

Further upstream, on the outside of a deep bend,

137

Nostos was catching dace on macaroni. He was using a vintage roach rod, sitting on his creel in the sun, puffing happily on his pipe and looking the absolute picture of piscatorial bliss. But his swim was obviously much too good for him and he was going to have to be turfed out after lunch to make way for a worthier angler.

Lunch! As if summoned by a mystical inner voice, fishermen began appearing from all along the river, each one heading purposefully towards the fishing hut. I only just got in before the last seat was taken. And what a spread it was! Arrayed on a large table were pies of every description, from the traditional to the exotic, a vast range of cheeses, many loaves and wine - enough to raise the river over its banks.

I sat opposite Bernard who had not cast a line all morning but had been happily walking the banks, enjoying the scenery and deciding where to fish later on. Bernard raised his glass and made a toast 'to Izaak Walton, thanking him for this pleasant day'. Izaak is our spiritual president and Birtwhistle Ford our ordinary president. Mr Ford made a toast 'to my 7lb chub'. But everyone ignored him as he was obviously becoming deranged.

Our club reel maker produced one of his latest creations and we passed it around as if we were handling the Crown Jewels. No one from any other walk of life appreciates their accoutrements so much as anglers, but no anglers drool over their tackle like the Golden Scale Club. The way we almost tremble when admiring a specially fine centrepin or an historic cane rod is almost pathetic.

Lunch over, the well fed, well juiced assembly went cheerfully back to where they'd left their tackle. One or two members, those who had been catching the most fish, discovered that their gear seemed to have mysteriously shifted a few yards up the bank. Even more curious was the fact that the tackle of other members, those who had not been catching any fish, had somehow materialised in the middle of these productive swims.

I was pleased to find that Bernard had pulled rank on Nostos and ousted him from his dace shoal, though he's such a gallant gentleman that I'm sure he allowed himself to be dragged perfectly gracefully from the riverbank. Bernard got a big dace first cast.

Demus Canning and Max the Pugilist had been getting some good chub earlier from 'miles downstream'. They returned that way after lunch, probably because they hadn't had as much wine as the rest of us.

I found a glorious looking swim, hemmed in by willows at the head of a slack side stream. Tackling up with a 13-foot Hardy 'Thames Style' roach rod and light float tackle, I began to fish. First cast, I hooked a nice roach, but unfortunately it got off at the net. After trickling in a few more maggots I cast again and once more, the float dunked under almost instantly. It wasn't a roach this time, but a pathetic 8oz eel which unfortunately did not get off. Two more such river worms followed before I finally hooked another roach. Unaccountably it rolled off at the net.

News reached me that Pikeater had got amongst a tremendous gudgeon shoal. Naturally we all abandoned our swims and hurried to his assistance, rods in hand. Gudgeon always make other species seem very ordinary, especially when they are in someone else's swim. But Pikeater was wearing chest waders and had reached a spot that was inaccessible to the rest of us. As we used to do when we were children and the person opposite was catching lots of fish, we began casting across to his swim. The current however, was too quick on our side and we couldn't control the lines, let alone our floats. By a fluke I caught a small chub, then a grayling, then a roach. But I couldn't attain to the more lordly gudgeon.

The afternoon doesn't last long at the end of the year and all too soon the sun was slanting into the distant woods and our floats were beginning to lose their colour. Within a few minutes, the first star had appeared and our floats were hardly visible at all on the dark surface. Time for tea, and we trudged back to the now lamplit hut, where the kettle was boiling and a sensational fruit cake was being cut into generous slices.

So ended another typical club outing. No monsters to rave about, yet it could hardly have been more enjoyable, even though no one fell in. No one was pushed in either. Only Pikeater wore that smug expression of a man who has caught gudgeon.

CHAPTER 25

Spectral Carp Fishing

This may be the last decade of the twentieth century, when technological advancement has made possible everything from space flight to instant mashed potato, but this has not made much difference to the world stock of mysteries. Despite our incredible wealth of knowledge, there are still countless secrets to unravel, still a thousand unanswered questions. I'm not simply talking about the Big Questions here, like the birth of the universe and the meaning of life; we still don't understand our own minds, our own dreams. Everyone can appreciate a mystery, though some folk get rather worried by such an undefined, vague subject. Personally, I'm always happy to enter into the spirit of these things.

Fishing takes us into an area where mysteries large and small happen all the time. Why was it, for instance, that the barbel in my favourite swim all began leaping and rolling in the middle of a cold winter's day last week, when I've never seen them leap there at all, except in the evening? But never on a winter evening. How did the carp I was stalking last summer simply vanish in front of me? It was in shallow margins, very big and clearly visible. I crept up and cast for it, dropping a single grain of freelined corn right next to it. It carried on quietly feeding, sending up the odd shower of bubbles. I glanced down to check the line on my reel and when I looked back, after about two seconds, the fish had somehow disappeared. Yet there was nowhere it could have gone without me seeing it as it had been thirty yards from any deep water. And there wasn't even a wave or a ripple to suggest it had gone anywhere.

And why, on another summer day this season, did I set off to one carp lake but then abruptly change course for another water where I'd never succeeded in catching a fish before? The carp in this other pool were big and very canny, but on that particular day I just knew, suddenly, that my luck was in. And it was.

Rivers, lakes and ponds can be very mysterious places in their own right and we can all respond differently to them, for a variety of reasons. A friend of mine loves the Dorset Stour because it is a warm hearted river, but he finds the Hampshire Avon cool and 'detached' and therefore hardly ever fishes it. I, on the other hand, prefer the Avon to the Stour, because I find the latter rather quiet and tame after the Avon's power and speed. And the atmosphere is different. Many people have commented on the strange atmosphere of Redmire Pool, and not all of them are carp anglers either. A trout-fishing friend of mine, who is also a friend of Redmire's owners, had his first ever look at the pool last autumn. 'What a weird spot it is!' he said. 'I've never felt such a sense of invisible presence before.'

But there is the same kind of unusual presence at many other quiet places like Redmire. It is not, I think, because of ghosts - whatever they might be. I believe there is a more complex, even more subtle explanation: something connected with the spirit of the place rather than the spirit of a personality and it has much to do with our own sensitivity towards our surroundings.

There was an old monastery pool that a friend of mine, Alan, and I once fished, twenty years ago. Meeting a few locals in the nearby pub before we set out, we were told to watch out for the old monk!

'What's it look like?' asked Alan. 'Like an old monk of course!' And they all laughed.

'Has he got any bad habits?' I asked and everyone groaned. I wanted someone to say quietly, 'but joking apart lads...' Yet no one had anything specific to say about this famous phantom. Probably, I thought, a poacher had once seen a man creeping past with a coat held up over his head because it was raining and so another legend had been born.

'Does he always patrol the banks, this ghost of yours?' I asked.

'No, never. He always crosses the pool in a boat.'

'Is it a real boat?' asked Alan.

'No, there has never been a boat here, at least not for as long as anyone can recall,' said the landlord.

It rained on the first night and we didn't get a sight of a carp or a ghost or anything. But then, the next day, the weather improved and we went back in the evening for another attempt. It was a beautiful pool, deep and dark, set in the middle of a wide grassy meadow and with dense oak woods and high hills all round. We began fishing by the one area of shallows, where a dense bed of lilies spread out from the margins. We tossed crusts along the edge of the lily bed and carp began to rise for them as it grew dark. Alan hooked a fish, but lost it in the pads. Then I hooked one, kept it in open water, but lost it at the net. No matter, there were obviously lots more carp to be caught as the violent slurpings and loud suckings demonstrated.

The night began to cool and a dense mist started to form across the water. Then the moon rose, adding another essential element to the scene. All we needed now was the dark silhouette of a hooded monk. But nothing else occurred, though it was curious that the carp suddenly stopped cavorting in the lilies. Everything became very quiet and we could watch more closely the way the mist gradually encroached from the water to the bankside, overflowing into the surrounding meadows like boiling milk spilling from a saucepan. After an hour or two it was impossible to see any of the pool at all; it appeared as if we were simply sitting in a cloud. We began to long for the dawn and the feel of the warm sun. We were getting rather chilly.

At around 2am, we heard a very strange sound. Initially I thought it must be a gigantic swan pushing powerfully across the pool towards us; there was that same slow rhythmic 'sloosh' that you hear when a swan is going to confront something. We hadn't previously noticed a swan on the pool, though, and then began to realise that it probably wasn't a swan anyway, it was more like the sound of oars. The slow, strong strokes rising and falling were definitely getting closer, louder, and we expected at any moment to see something unearthly materialising out of the mist. But nothing appeared and there was just that rhythmic wash of water that abruptly stopped, right in front of us. Then, as before, complete silence. Nothing else happened. We said nothing. We did nothing. It was superbly inexplicable.

CHAPTER 26

Things that go Weird in the Night

Fishing is a chancy business. It wouldn't be nearly so enjoyable if it wasn't. No angler, no matter how good, can always catch fish, but conversely, no fish, no matter how cunning, will always resist temptation. There comes a day in even the cleverest fish's life when he goes a bit daft and picks up the nearest hook bait. And because fishing is a game of chance, ruled as much by luck as skill, there is every possibility that the bait he picks up will be yours.

Angling wouldn't be fun at all if we could always predict what was going to happen, if we all fished in standardised ponds, each stocked with the standardised fish

147

providing standardised entertainment with no danger of surprise, disappointment or too much excitement. The idea of the angling theme park fills me with horror. It inspires a vision of hell where every fishery is either commercially or charity sponsored, where everything is artificial and even the fish are not allowed to break the rules.

Fishing reaffirms our links with the natural world, a world that is still full of mysteries and genuine beauty, a world which we instinctively respond to simply because it has made us what we are. And because fishing offers so much potential you need unconditional freedom to explore all of its possibilities. You have to be sensitive and responsible, of course, but to get the best out of fishing you have to interpret it in your own terms while always keeping intact the hint of wildness that is the original attraction of angling.

That wildness, which your angling theme park would suffocate, is still the essential attraction for me. It is a quality of natural disorder that makes for those chance happenings of good and bad luck. And however sceptical you are, it is that natural disorder that continues to provide countless episodes that puzzle, mystify or amuse. For instance, I was recently entertained by the comical but marvellous sight of a big eel following the tail of a 20 lb carp, while the carp followed the tail of the eel. I was high in a tree, overlooking the shallows of a local lake and the two unlikely partners danced a slow, graceful pirouette

148

together for several minutes before the carp lost interest and drifted languidly away.

Even more amusing was the scene of three horses drinking together at the margins of a lake when a carp leapt into the air only ten feet away from them. It was a big fish and it made a big splash, causing the horses to rear up and bolt in panic. And while the horses thundered off, the carp and several of its companions bolted in the opposite directions, trailing great waves across the surface.

Curious incidents like these are happening all the time. You just have to keep your eyes open to notice them though sometimes you can even have your eyes shut, like the time when I was dozing against a tree one night, waiting for a carp to bite, and I felt rather than heard something sniffing at my left ear. It took me a moment to come properly to my senses, then I realised it was a badger. I leapt to my feet but the animal didn't panic and just shambled noisily away into the moonlight.

A similar incident, but much stranger, occurred at the most peculiar place I've ever fished, the Evening Pitch or Old Boathouse Pitch on the east bank of Redmire Pool. You hear some fairly weird tales if you spend much time with habitual night anglers, and the spookiest of these all concern the Evening Pitch. Even the most unimaginative, down-to-earth fishermen could have their nerves jangled by some inexplicable happening. These could include disembodied voices, sudden changes of tempera-

149

ture, an electrifying sharpening of the senses, a shadowy figure or (almost too much of a cliché this one) a luminous, staring face. I never saw anything there, even though I would often choose to fish there at night, especially when I was alone, simply so I might learn something about the mystery. Regularly, I would be aware of a gradually nearing presence, but because I was fishing Redmire, I would often put this down to an instinctive recognition of a big carp passing close by.

Once, I heard a terrific shout that made me leap even higher than when I was sniffed by the badger – and yet there was no one else at the pool that night. It was as if someone had yelled directly into my ear.

All these incidents culminated in a terrific scare when the owner of Redmire and his son were camping in a tent in the Evening Pitch. They woke suddenly in the night to that staring, luminous face. And though I still think it might merely have been a carp angler looking for his lost boilies, they had such a fright that – according to my information – they arranged for a service or exorcism.

It conjures quite a dramatic scene – *The Exorcist Visits Redmire!* Yet, whatever your belief I can't accept that a human agency, however divinely inspired, has a monopoly over the world's mysteries. Seven years after the attempt to lay the unquiet spirit to rest, the Evening Pitch is still haunted.

These things concern the background to fishing,

but there are just as many baffling or curious incidents that are more directly connected. I was once fishing for perch with my brother Nick and a friend, Guy. We were sitting in a line on the bank, waiting for one of our floats to move. Suddenly, both Nick and Guy's floats dipped simultaneously. They both hooked the same half-pound perch. The same thing happened to another pal of mine, Mark Walsingham, when he was fishing the River Isle in Somerset. He had a bite and struck at the same moment the angler on the far bank had a bite. Up to the surface came a very unlucky gudgeon. Mark had hooked if fairly, the other angler had hooked it in the tail.

Non-anglers who presume that all fish suffer and die after capture should be persuaded differently. Their opinions would certainly change if they were more aware of the many repeat captures of particular specimens. But they would probably not have been any more surprised than I was if they'd witnessed what happened following my release of a ten pound mirror carp recently. I'd caught the fish in the dark and as it was a lovely looking creature. I wanted a photograph of it when the sun came up. So I carefully sacked the fish and got my picture four hours later. During the interval the carp must have built up quite an appetite. Seconds after I let it go the indicator went up on my rod and I hooked it again, fair and square, on the same bait.

The rod-maker, Shaun Linsley will recall the time when he netted a 7lb barbel for me on the Hampshire Avon, released it some yards downstream, then jumped into my swim before I could say Spam. But it was a good, productive swim. I'd had a fish and it was only fair that he should get one too. So while Shaun expectantly cast, I slowly fished my way upstream towards the next bend.

Perhaps twenty minutes passed and just as I was trundling a sliver of luncheon meat through a dense weed bed, I had a solid thump of a bite and hooked another barbel. But then I discovered it wasn't another fish. It was the same seven-pounder, no question about it as it had an identifiable scar and a clear distinguishing feature on one of its barbules. It had taken the same bait in the same manner, but from a place well upstream of its previous release point.

Hugh Miles, who made the film *A Passion for Angling* for BBC TV, is an obsessive and extremely good roach angler. But when we were filming the barbel catching sequence in which the young angler, Peter, lands an eight-pounder, Hugh suddenly decided he wanted to catch a barbel too. The swim we'd baited was full of them and on the day after filming, before anyone else had arrived on the river, Hugh crept into position and began to fish with sweetcorn. By the time I'd got there, the fish were feasting enthusiastically on Hugh's groundbait, but he'd not yet even had a bite. There were about a dozen good barbel clearly visible under his rod point and four medium sized chub. Suddenly, his rod-tip pulled gently around, Hugh struck and in came a 1lb roach. 'That's impossible,' he said. Later that day, as we were scouting along a quiet, lily-covered back water, we found a nice group of carp and I got a 9lb mirror first cast, again on sweetcorn. We tossed in some more attractors and within ten minutes the carp were back.

Now Hugh crept forward, having decided it was his turn for a rod-bender. He dropped in a hook-full of corn, the line swung instantly taut and in came... another 1lb roach. 'You can't keep a good roach angler down,' I said. 'Even when there weren't any roach around in the first place.'

A different kind of incident, but no less peculiar, took place on the last Saturday of last season. It was a mild March day, with the Avon fining down just right for an 11th hour barbel. I was fishing with Jeff Greene and we hoped we might make up for our previous run of completely blank days. In fact, up until then, the year had not provided us with a single Avon barbel. I cast into a new and likely-looking swim and had a wonderful bite first run down with a rolling leger. Of course, I missed it. I cast again and, as the bait approached the hot spot, I tensed, ready to strike. There wasn't a definite bite, but the tackle stopped in mid-roll with the current zithering across the line, and I struck.

Something swung down with the powerful flow and swept under the submerged willow immediately below me. It clogged instantly up in the branches, but when I wound myself downstream I could see the fish in about six

153

foot of water, tied up in the twigs. I whistled loudly and Jeff soon arrived with the long-handled landing net.

'First barbel of the year,' I said. 'Don't mess it up or you'll go in after it.'

He nearly went in anyway as he had to climb precariously out into the willow before he could reach the fish. Amazingly, he got it in the mesh first swipe and with much jubilation I helped him back onto dry land with our prize. But suddenly our laughter stopped. The barbel was dead and had obviously been so for at least a week. It was only the cold water that had stopped it from going off. Somehow, I'd foul hooked it in the top of the head and the strong current had bowled it downstream making it feel alive. Dour, but alive.

We buried the fish under an elder tree behind us and went off downstream to try somewhere else.

'Done any good?' asked another angler as we passed him by.

'Well,' I said. 'There's a barbel hole upstream where I could guarantee you would find a fish, but it's gone a bit dead for the moment.'

A Lucky Star

I first fished at Breamore on the Hampshire Avon in
October 1996 and there was a noticeable difference
between the river there and the more familiar stretches
downstream. It seemed slightly wilder, more unkempt,
more attractive because of that. There were signs that it
had once been made to behave itself more politely, but was
now shaking off its stultifyingly good manners. The hatches
on the weirpool had been washed away long ago and the
timber shuttering and deflectors along the bank were disap-
pearing into vegetation. There were choked up carriers and
marshes that made a paradise for frogs and grass snakes.
The flood meadows on either side were rough and tussocky,
much to the liking of the local avians: on that first day I saw

amongst dozens of the more common birds, a peregrine, several buzzards, three different kingfishers, a cettis warbler and a barn owl. Though it was autumn, the water crowfoot was still green and dense and in the gravel runs between the long tresses I saw salmon, dace, roach, chub, trout and – what I was really looking for – barbel. I saw four on that first day: two of them were only small, one was a middleweight and the biggest appeared just after sunset on the end of my line, a bristling, bright golden specimen of 8lb 12oz.

On the following Monday I went again, taking Jeff Greene along with me. He had been intrigued by my earlier description of the place and, with my old V.W. dead at dawn, had offered me the use of his Nissan as long as he could bring his barbel rod. It was a clear, mild day with hardly a movement in the air. We walked upstream from the bridge and went to have a look at the weirpool. There was only one other person in sight, a woman fishing for chub just below the outfall. She hadn't had any fish but, she said, she couldn't complain, what with the weather so fine and the river looking perfect.

We had a walk upstream, but couldn't find any barbel, just a few big chub and a recently-arrived salmon. When we got back to the weir the lady chubber had gone and we decided we liked the look of the place she'd been casting to. Baiting with pink indispensable, using 8lb b.s. line on our centrepins and 11ft cane rods, we searched that side of the weir all afternoon but didn't even get a peck from an eel. At sunset I fished my way several hundred yards along the upstream bank, but yet again, despite those wonderful conditions, I couldn't even will a response.

Over in the east, the moon came up above the edge of the New Forest, just before the sun finally disappeared into the west. The temperature began to drop, but not too alarmingly, and I walked back through the twilight and decided to fish the last hour at the weir. Ken the keeper had, the previous week, told me there was a tremendous head of barbel in the weirpool. It was late autumn, the time of the year when barbel regularly de-mystify themselves. The river was in ideal condition and it was that magical hour of the day when all species begin to lose a little natural caution. Furthermore, while the barbel fisher is almost universally frustrated along most of the Avon, forced by petty local rules to abandon his swim during that most propitious time, on the Breamore stretch we could, if we liked, fish till sunrise. Just that prospect alone made us as gleeful as if we'd caught a netful.

Jeff, the saviour of many otherwise hungry days, brewed up a final pot of tea, which he served with a generous slab of buttered fruit loaf. Then a man appeared in the garden of the millhouse opposite and lit a bonfire. The smoke spiralled straight up while, at the same time, a thin mist began to rise from the river.

His tea finished, Jeff went to have a few casts

157

upstream and while he was gone I saw a spectacular meteorite falling vertically towards the eastern horizon. It was so brilliant it woke the slumbering moorhens and made them cluck in alarm. I counted two seconds, which is a very long time for a meteorite. Its reflection in the weir tail made me stare that way for some while even after it had gone. Obviously an omen.

I told Jeff what he'd missed when he returned and he too felt it must have been an omen. So I began to fish my way downstream, although Jeff walked right round and cast directly into the weir tail. He is always so much more decisive than me and so, after a short while, he became aware that I was materialising from the reed bed next to him. Immediately I knew we'd been in the wrong place all day. Everything suddenly felt right. Jeff was standing, casting slightly downstream to his left, I sat on my creel and cast slightly upstream. I saw the little moonlit splash as the lead hit the water. Within minutes, just as I was inching the bait back towards me, there was a slight tremor of life, then a pluck. I jagged at it, but merely pulled in a hookful of weed stems. Yet it *had* been a bite. I cast again to exactly the same spot, let the tackle settle, inched it through a deep weedbed and felt it settle again on clear gravel. I waited less than a minute before the rod was pulled decisively over.

Ah! Wondrous contact! How satisfying it was. The Avocet went into a nice trembling arc and I looked appreciatively at its silhouette against the moonlight. 'It's probably a chub,' I said. Just in case.

It simply jogged leisurely about for a while, but kept close enough to the riverbed to convince me it definitely wasn't a chub. I slowed it finally, or it got bored, and I gradually and very gently eased it towards me. However it wasn't going to play my game and suddenly locked itself away in a weedbed. The rod became locked also, lifeless and static, and increasing its bend made no difference. I began to get nervous. Moving a few yards to the right and tightening up the line a few octaves, I finally lifted anchor and the fish sailed out into open water. Twenty yards away there was a glinting swirl on the surface. The rod point was dragged down towards it and the barbel surged away so slowly and so relentlessly that I had to keep adjusting my imagination to make room for it. The fish seemed to travel a tremendous distance before it slowed and stopped, wallowing invisibly. I wound down, turned it and tried to keep the subsequent retrieve absolutely even and unwavering. Jeff came up next to me with the net and we could see a moon-glinting bow wave coming gradually towards us. We could even see the light along the line. The fish began to sweep past us along the bankside sedge, but Jeff somehow managed to lean out far enough to get the barbel to plough straight into the mesh. He started to lift, but stuck halfway and had to drag the fish through the stems and onto the bank. Gently, I lifted it up and it looked enormous. But moonlight can be deceptive. Its scales gleamed coldly, its great fins flared, its head looked as big as a labrador's.

It was absurdly important that we put definite numbers to it – 32 inches long, 12lb 10oz in weight. I'd never caught a twelve pounder before so I went home feeling more than happy about life and the universe and perfectly convinced about the significance of falling stars.

CHAPTER 28

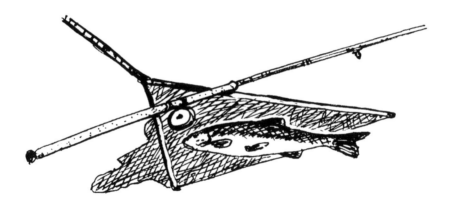

The Black Swan

Even when he's not catching anything, the optimistic angler can never fail. On his fishing ledger, the interest rates increase by around ten per cent for each blank day. It's a wonderful system.

My nine previous river trips had not been entirely successful, but my lack of withdrawals therefore raised the value of the next fish I was going to catch. In fact even a baby chub was going to be worth its weight in gold. So, as the weather had become soft and still after days of cold winds, rain and even snow, I headed again for the middle reaches of the Hampshire Avon, my optimism higher than it had been all season.

It had rained heavily the previous night and by early afternoon, when I reached the river, the level was beginning to rise and the water was beginning to cloud. But the colour did not have that sour greenish tinge of snow-melt, nor the dirty brown that marks a sudden end to a dry period. It was a good, clear, winter chalkstream colour. I headed upstream, passing a weirpool that had a much bigger voice than when I last heard it. I followed a line of bank-side alders and spotted a pair of green waders poking out from behind one of them. As I approached, the sound of a whistling kettle began to drown the now distant roar of the weir. I'd obviously arrived at the perfect moment. Jeff Greene was making tea.

We sat against the tree, holding our steaming tea mugs, watching the lively river and happily talking about all the barbel we were going to catch. It was the kind of conversation that all anglers have when they are in familiar company, on a familiar stretch of river and the conditions are just about ideal. By the time we'd finished our second mug (and eaten a very fine fruit cake) we were confidently predicting a new barbel record by sunset.

Eventually, Jeff cast into his swim and I wandered upstream to a deep underbank slack where, on my last visit, I'd seen a big fish roll. It looked even better than before, with the extra flow giving the slack a more clearly defined shape, making it easier to recognise the best spot to place a bait. I tackled up with a nice lissome two-piece rod (a Barder *Merlin*) and coupled it with a Dragonfly reel loaded with an 8lb line. I wanted to fish a fairly stationary bait, so threaded a $\frac{3}{4}$oz bomb directly onto the line, stopping it with a swan-shot. Hook was a No.6 eyed, and bait was hog-standard luncheon meat. Casting to the upstream edge of the slack gave me a little jag of a bite after only a few minutes. It came again within a few minutes more, but though I was expecting it, I missed on the strike.

Chub? Barbel? Big chub are the canniest of biters, but then I thought it was probably just an eel, his appetite roused by the rising temperature. Half an hour later, as I was trickling the bait a yard further down the slack, I felt another gentle pluck and this time I connected. The rod top went over and for a moment I felt that lovely savage thrill that you always feel when you first make contact. But then the pressure changed and the rod went all wobbly. Just as I thought – it was only an eel; it had felt like a proper fish because I'd somehow foul hooked it in its middle!

I slipped it back to continue its miraculous journey and decided to fish my way back to the weir. There were a couple of good looking pools to try downstream and perhaps I could also see how Jeff was getting on and maybe persuade him to get the kettle going again. But when I reached his swim, he wasn't there. Perhaps he'd thought about the weir too. Naturally, I had to have a quick cast into his bit of river. I've learnt that a recently vacated swim often produces a fish – one that is ripe for a different kind of bait or presentation. But not this time. Perhaps my feelings of optimism had been unfounded. Every pool along the river looked brimful of promise, yet those seductive expressions had completely deceived me.

A shadow of something slid into view from upstream. I turned and watched an elegant black swan drift towards me. It had been years since I'd seen a black swan on the Avon. Though I do not actually like ordinary swans very much – such tyrants – there is an extra quality of beauty in a black one. I took him as a good sign. He hesitated as he came level with me. He looked me straight in the eye, but not with a pleading give-me-a-bit-of-bread stare. It was more like a confirmation of something. Without moving a feather or a webbed foot, he just let the current take him away out of sight, downstream, towards the weir. It was obviously the direction to follow.

Midwinter afternoons don't last very long and by the time I'd reached the weirpool it was dark and the moon – a full moon – was rising up over the New Forest behind me. The breeze, which had been quite strong earlier, had died down and on that clear evening, the temperature hadn't dropped. Everything seemed even more perfect than before.

I was right about Jeff: the weir had lured him as well. There he was, fishing the left hand swing of the weir tail. I'd already decided to cast along the right hand swirl, and as I baited my hook, I realized we were in exactly the same positions as we had been when we'd fished there the previous year. Furthermore, although it was October then and December now, conditions were exactly the same, even

164

down to the full moon rising behind us. And then, of course, there had also been the Omens. The result of our last year's incident was my biggest ever barbel and now here we were again and I was absurdly confident that history would repeat itself. In fact I said to Jeff that any fish we caught would only be counted if it weighed over 12lb. But then I remembered that though we had fished the weirpool a number of times under different conditions, Jeff still hadn't caught a barbel from it. Therefore, it was really his turn. I was certain the fish were in front of me and suggested we change places. But he refused to move and though I thought I should drag him away from where the fish were not, I was selfish enough not to try.

To reach the part of the backflow I was aiming at required a long cast off the reel and, typically, I overdid it, overran the reel and got into an extravagant bird's nest. The bait dropped well short of its target and I spent several minutes unravelling the tangle. At one point I almost snapped the line in frustration, but everything finally pulled free and as I wound up the slack and raised the rod, something whammed it back down again. Then the reel began to sing my favourite song and a barbel – definitely a barbel – made a long steady drive diagonally across the pool. Even when it passed through the main surge it didn't veer to the side or slow down. 'Wow!' I said. 'This is, um, well, a big fish!'

After an age, I worked it all the way back, now zigzagging, now holding firm on the bottom, now thrashing the surface just off the reedbed where I was standing. Jeff leaned out with the net and, in the moonlight, we saw a large head surfacing just a yard beyond the frame. I drew it steadily towards us and Jeff lifted when the bulk of the fish seemed to be well over the mesh. But it was bigger than we thought – longer anyway, and it just slid back into the river. Then, its urge to flee made stronger by the sight of our two eager faces, it swept round and made a furious run down the weir tail. With the extra power of the current I just couldn't even slow it and had to race down after it, leaping a barbed wire fence and hoping I could at least get level with it before it reached the line of trees downstream. Once there, I wouldn't be able to follow it further and if it got beyond them and under the bridge, I'd probably lose it for sure. Amazingly, I managed to get in front of the fish and my downstream pull persuaded it back upstream, away from danger. I forced it into a tiny slack under a high bank, but, with the main surge so close, I shouted to Jeff that I couldn't hold it there for long. 'So get down here with the net before I lose my cool!'

Actually, I'd lost my cool as soon as it took off on its second run, but I was quite enjoying the atmosphere of near panic. I was leaning over the bankside fence but Jeff had to clamber over it to get down to the fish and in doing so, the mesh got nicely snagged in the barbed wire. In the moonlit darkness the panic rose to near hysteria before he'd freed it. Then, not realising how low I was holding the rod, he whammed it with the net and gave the barbel enough inches of slack for it to push into the current again. I got the rod-top right over and managed to swing it round in a tight arc back towards the net. With one smooth sweep, Jeff got it and heaved it up, over the fence and gently down onto the damp bankside grass.

As we unparcelled it from the mesh the moonlight caught its flank and made each individual scale gleam wonderfully. Of course it might just have been the moon, but it did look tremendous. It was definitely 10lb plus, but it didn't appear quite as long as last year's big fish. Different body shape, different dimensions; deeper, thicker and the fins not quite so large. Yet it was almost the same weight. The scales registered 12lb 6oz.

CHAPTER 29

First Day Intuition

Anyone reading the usual press reports after the opening of the season would think he was stunningly incompetent if he'd blanked. The pages of the angling papers trumpet forth the news that every fisherman and woman in the country enjoyed sensational catches, even if they'd stayed in bed. No doubt the first day of the season can be rewarding, with the fish having almost forgotten the meaning of the figure with the rod. But if the conditions are poor, say with a stiff chill wind and cold rain, then, as always in such circumstances, you'll be lucky to catch anything. Nevertheless, even if it's snowing, the idea of that first fish and the renewal of your contact with the magical under-water world, is very compelling. A fine fish on opening day is an idea that will probably happen, one day, but it shouldn't spoil things if it doesn't. The best thing about

169

June 16th is simply the return to your favourite reality.

The opening days were fairly typical for me. On the previous June 15th, the weather was beautifully hot, with just enough breeze to push the carp I was after up into some weedy shallows, where they began to feed earnestly. By midnight there were four members of the Golden Scale Club strung out along those shallows, all keenly expectant, not even thinking about making the traditional Opening Night Fanfare (with bugles and bicycle pumps). We'd been watching the carp feeding for four hours and we were certain we were in for a famous and truly glorious June 16th.

But the great fishing God, Izaak, decided we were being far too serious. We were behaving like common specimen hunters! So he had a little joke with us and swung the night wind suddenly right round from south to north and made it very strong and cold. Then he added a nice deluge of cold rain, just to ensure the carp would flee into the deepest, most inaccessible places in the lake. Unprepared for such a turn of events, we had no water-proofs or even any warm clothing. Luckily Jasper Tucker had a brolly and we crowded under it, trying to set ourselves on fire while we brewed endless pots of tea and waited for the dawn to arrive. If you're going to blank on June 16th, it's best to do it in style.

The following year was not dissimilar except that the approaching deadline for a TV series, *A Passion For*

Angling, meant that the traditional opening night with the Golden Scale Club had to be cancelled. The producer, Hugh Miles, wanted to film the capture of a record carp and so I had to be at a secret location at first light, ready for an historic occasion. We hadn't even got the rods ready before the heavens opened and began to wash away any thoughts of serious fishing.

Just like the previous year, I sheltered from the weather and drank endless cups of tea, though this time I was more comfortable as we had Hugh's camper parked by the waterside. If it had been warm as well as wet it would have been worth fishing, even though the light was grey and gloomy; but it was really cold and by lunchtime we knew that the carp weren't going to play till the summer came back.

'It's no good,' said Hugh, who is, to be honest, keener on angling than film-making, 'I'm going tench fishing instead.' So everybody went their separate ways. I went home thereby amazing my loving family, who never expect me back early from fishing, especially on the first day of the season. As I sat down for a late lunch, the phone rang. It was Shaun Linsley.

'I'm in the pub,' he said. 'By the Long Lake. You'd better come over. The carp are just beginning to move.'

'How did you know I'd be home?' I asked. 'Well, I guessed you wouldn't be filming in this weather and presumed you'd run for cover.'

171

'OK,' I said, 'I'll see you over there later this after-noon – earlier if it stops raining.'

It didn't stop. In fact it got heavier. Then it was tea time and I had another excuse not to go out and risk a drowning. Finally, just when everyone here was happily thinking I'd be around to read them a bedtime story, the rain stopped, and even the sun came out. Perhaps I'd go fishing after all.

I got in the steamed-up car (naturally all my wet tackle was still in the back) and drove off towards the Long Lake. However, after about a mile, I suddenly decided I couldn't possibly meet Shaun. Despite what he'd said, I wasn't optimistic about that place and, anyway, I'd suddenly realised that if I went off to another different lake, I would definitely catch a carp. Though I know I often go on about these moments of absolute certainty, when everything in the world leads inexorably towards some outsize fish, they don't actually happen very often. However, when they do, there is no denying them and though I never alter my technique or baits, they never fail. What was interesting about this particular experience was the fact that I was driving unexpectedly towards a lake where I'd never succeeded before. It was a lake of big carp, but also of uninterrupted blanks.

The evening sun was on the bankside trees as I crept down to the water. It looked a different world compared to the one I'd been waiting in, twelve hours earlier. This was the kind of June 16th we all dream about, with the lake hushed and expectant and the air full of strange enchantment. But where were the carp? I crept out from the shallows and down almost to the dam; there wasn't a sign of fish anywhere, no bubbles, swirls or even vague puffs of disturbed silt. Was my instinct playing me false?

I was beginning to have insidious little doubts about the whole adventure. At least if I'd gone to the Long Lake I could have ended up in the pub with Shaun and toasted yet another glorious blank. But then, at the last pitch before the dam, I stared down again into the deep crystal clear water and saw, right in the margins, an indistinct blue-ish form gradually materialise into a carp. Not only a carp, but a common carp, a mid-20; the perfect creature to say 'Hello' to on opening day. I flicked it three grains of corn on a size 8, freelined, and it took them instantly but blew them out again just as instantly. Then it went round in a big slow circle and came directly back to the bait. Because of the reflections, I couldn't see clearly what happened next, but I noticed the line cutting very slowly from left to right and the fish drifting the same way. So I struck and connected.

There was a big flash of gold eight feet down, then the carp rushed straight towards an ancient, half-submerged tree. I was using was a marvellous old carp rod, made by Richard Walker 40 years previously. It hooped over

173

dramatically, but its superbly seasoned fibres still had more than enough power to swerve the carp off course. Amid violent upswirls and downswirls, flying spray, clouds of bubbles and disturbed mud, I managed to keep the fish circling until I could persuade it into the net. It was a lovely fish, very dark along the back, but with the gold scales, almost silvery edged, as if the flanks were meshed with twilight. And it weighed just over twenty-two pounds.

What had been a disappointing first day was made memorable, not so much because of the fish's size, but because it confirmed my sudden intuition.

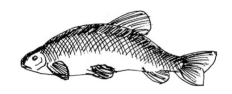

CHAPTER 30

A Ditch in Time

The Mole at Mickelham is a pretty stretch of river, flowing around the steep chalk escarpment of Boxhill before winding its way northward along a deep wooded valley towards Leatherhead.

In the early '60s, when I made my first explorations along its banks, the surface was often flecked with shoals of dace and small chub. The larger specimens were less easy to find, but by creeping under or climbing into overhanging trees, I soon realised where they were hiding.

All my earliest angling experiences had been on still waters and river fishing presented a very different challenge, one that, for a whole season, I was not equal to. But gradually I began to get into the flow of things, learning that, while location of fish was much easier in the river's transparent depths than in the murk of my familiar ponds, presentation of bait was more difficult and more important. I couldn't just cast a float and wait for a bite – I had to learn to use the current, to work the bait and yet make it appear natural as it approached the fish.

There was never any consistency in my catches but at least my expectations slowly rose from minnows towards grander heights. I caught perch, dace, small chub and occasionally bigger chub. Some of them weighed nearly a pound! My angling pals, who had been happy to remain by their ponds, were so staggered by these catches that they decided to come with me to the river and share its wonders.

Privately, I don't really think they believed the whole truth of my stories and there was definitely an air of 'O.K. let's see one of these big fish, then!' when we first arrived there. Luckily, the fish were in an obliging mood that day and not only could I show them several amazing monsters lurking beneath sunken willow boughs, I also caught a half-pound dace which was twice the size of anything we'd managed back at the ponds. (We may have dreamt of carp, but all we ever caught were gudgeon and little perch). Unfortunately, I couldn't rise to a chub as well, but my pals – Peter, Derek and Dave – saw enough to convince themselves of the wisdom of river fishing.

We began to make regular visits, going first by bicycle and then, aggravated by the many vertical hills, switching to the train, which was a much more leisurely experience. Meeting at Epsom, we'd buy a ticket to Westhumble and the journey always had a nice sense of anticipation as we talked about the great fish waiting at the end of it. There was also the added delight of rattling along the river for the last few miles and eventually crossing it as we came into the station. From Westhumble it was only a short walk down to the Stepping Stones. We'd hop over them and then fish our way slowly downstream towards Burford Bridge and sometimes beyond.

The fishing was free – or at least we never discovered otherwise – but this often meant that, especially on August weekends, there was fierce competition for the best swims. Mid-week was the favoured time, though it was during one of these quieter periods that we had a run-in with the most competitive anglers we had ever met.

Peter, Derek and I had spent the morning fishing a deep pool below a little footbridge. Nothing much had been caught – the usual minnows, a gudgeon and a small dace – but, because it was the place where, according to history, someone had once caught a two-pound perch, we thought we should persevere till tea-time.

At noon we took a break from fishing and went off to climb some trees in the woods. We weren't gone long, though I do remember that we tried to get to the top of a very tall beech and someone got his foot stuck in a forked branch causing much hilarity, vertigo and panic. When we got back to our swim, our rods and duffle bags had been thrown up the bank and two mean looking elders (say, fifteen or sixteen) were casting for our fish. They didn't even turn round when Derek said, 'This is our spot.' And we waited for some seconds before one of them grunted quietly, 'Not any more, it's not.'

'But we've been here all morning,' I pleaded.

'Then you've been here long enough,' mumbled the spokesman, again without turning to face us.

Peter, Derek and I looked at one another, trying to decide whether to do something heroic. It was obvious that reason was not going to get us anywhere. But then the one who hadn't spoken turned round and gave us such a calmly murderous look that all ideas of direct action fled.

'Push off!' he spat, and turned back to his fishing.

We were twelve and thirteen year old flyweights. These two were heavyweights. It was true we outnumbered them, but we also guessed that if we made any move against them they'd simply mince us up for groundbait.

They ignored us completely as we collected our bits and pieces and trooped disconsolately away down the bank. When we got to the footbridge we agreed that, firstly, we couldn't fish any more because, secondly, we couldn't let them get away with it. Crossing the bridge from the field side, we climbed up the wooded slopes opposite, then sneaked along between the trees until we were level with our persecutors. We were a long way above them, but also about fifty yards back from the water's edge. We didn't have our catapults, but we were all quite good at throwing stones, especially me, who, despite having the build of a grasshopper, had a kind of whip-hand action which could send a pebble out of sight. In fact, a good stone throwing arm is still my only physical boast.

One moment the two thugs were grunting contentedly over their stolen pool, the next they were bellowing with rage as a salvo of flint and chalk came raining into the water in front of them. I saved my best stone till the third throw and it dooshed down so close to the far bank that the spray caught them both. Dropping their rods, they raced down to the footbridge, going much faster than we'd expected.

'Split up,' said Peter. 'See you back at the station.'

He ran up the hill, Derek vanished into the trees and I hurried along the river, heading towards Burford Bridge. I found myself on a footpath, which was good for speed but no good for concealment and I was nearly spotted as the two bloodsuckers came swarming up from below. With their ghastly yells getting louder in my ears, I leaped down the slope through a thicket of box trees and found myself on the riverbank again! I scampered along until I came to a very narrow chalky ditch overhung with dense yew branches. It was obvious that my pursuers were gaining on me, but the box trees had briefly obscured me giving me just a moment's opportunity to slip unseen into the ditch, dragging my rod and bag behind me. I crawled along it under the matted branches and lay still, though my heart was thumping.

The murderers were upon me in a few seconds but they never even hesitated. They jumped the ditch and pounded on up the bank towards the bridge. I didn't hesitate either. I slid out from my cover and bolted back downstream heading now for the Stepping Stones and freedom.

An hour later Peter, Derek and I were on the train home, laughing and whooping.

But we decided not to fish the river again for a week or two.

CHAPTER 31

Just Desserts

I was at peace. The afternoon was calm and warm, the woodpigeons were murmuring sleepily in the trees and the lake was spread out before me like a luminous carpet. Beneath this surface tranquillity were the tranquil carp, but they weren't going to do anything other than bask in the sun and I wasn't expecting any disturbances at all, especially as I had not even cast yet. I would just quietly wait, watch and doze until the atmosphere changed.

     There were other anglers sharing my sanctuary - it was, after all, a club lake and the summer holidays meant that keen young carp fishers often made the epic bike ride across Thursley Common to try for a monster. I could hear distant voices and knew that a couple of young anglers were fishing a popular and productive pitch between the lily beds just across a bay from me. But they were keeping their voices as quiet as their excitement would allow and they weren't disturbing me. After about an hour, though, in fact just after I'd made my first (free) offering to the fish, the voices suddenly became louder and harsher.

They've hooked a carp! I thought, but then I realised something else was happening. There were older voices mingled in with the other two and it sounded as though they were arguing quite angrily. I was irritated at first, then I tried to imagine what they were arguing about, then I couldn't stand it any more and went to see what the fuss was about. Walking round from the north to the west bank I was confronted by two very disconsolate young fisherboys. They were about twelve or thirteen walking towards me with their heads hung down and their rods and tackle almost dragging along the ground behind them. When I asked them what the trouble was they replied that two carp anglers had arrived in their pitch and claimed it was theirs as they had baited it up the previous evening. When the youngsters said that wasn't fair and no-one could baggy a pitch if they weren't already in it, the two senior interlopers threatened them.

'We didn't come here to have a fight,' said one of them. 'We just want to fish in peace.' said the other. I thought about reinstating them after trying to persuade the invaders to move on, but I felt this would just create more bad feeling and possibly make the place more hostile for the boys in the future. I had a better idea.

First I went to see the two newcomers. I didn't recognise them and I obviously didn't like them. They were crunching about on the bank making enough disturbance to scare every fish in the area. I had a word with them - just the one. It described them perfectly. Then I went back to where the youngsters were waiting. 'Come and see these fish,' I said.

The previous week I had the carp bubbling wildly over a bait they'd not sniffed before - racing pigeon peas, cooked in paprika. It had such a good effect, I landed a twenty pounder almost instantly.

As I hoped, the fish were beginning to move again and after advising the boys to simplify their tackle - to use plasticine on their line instead of clumping lead weights - we baited their hooks with bird beans and they cast out.

Expectations were high, and spirits were rising again, but I became impatient and even concerned after half an hour with the lines still untwitched. The carp were plainly evident, bubbling once more over the scattered offerings, but they were being far too canny about the hookbaits.

We needn't have worried. Another few minutes slipped by, then the right hand line cut up suddenly through the surface film and the response caused a wonderful splash and a great surging bow wave. The carp headed straight for the lilies across the bay.

'Don't hold it too hard!' I warned. 'The lilies aren't too bad. If it gets in, you can easily get it out again.'

It didn't quite get in the pads, anyway. There was a tremendous eruption just short of them, but by then the fish had already travelled over fifty yards. Its first rush was over.

Much to my delight it then walloped and crashed at the end of that long line, right in front of the two pitch thieves. We shouted a lot and made it very plain what was happening, though we went over the top a little which would have been unfortunate if the carp had got off. But we landed it safely in the end.

'What a fish!' the boys whooped, and I thought they might be over-revving again, to make the other two think it was much bigger than it was.

It was a twelve pound common, which was actually much smaller than I was expecting after such a spectacular scrap. Then I remembered what I would have felt like at their age if I'd caught such a fish. Their elation was absolutely genuine.

After they'd cycled off home, an hour or two later, I went round to see what was happening elsewhere on the lake. I glanced in the direction of the two invaders, but they were no longer there and we never saw them again.

CHAPTER 32

Paradise Withheld

As we came through the last line of trees and onto the bank, we both made the same kind of long drawn-out exclamation.

'Wowww...'

What a place! We wanted to become part of it.

It was a large lake in a wooded valley. There were extensive lily beds, overgrown islands and a mossy old boathouse gently sinking into a reedy bay. It was ancient and neglected, but the water had that vivid transparency that always reveals the existence of either deep springs or a healthy inlet stream. And there were obviously plenty of our favourite species.

The lily pads were jostling mysteriously as carp ploughed slowly between the stems. There were patches of silvery bubbles that we knew were carp bubbles. And then, as a final confirmation, a magical golden creature rose up from the depths, stood on its tail for a slow second and then crashed back. The wheeling ripples spread towards us, transfixing us. Guy and I had seen this lake in a picture in a book, had found it on a map and had now come to investigate. It was even better than we'd imagined, but we knew that before we could fish it, we would have to seek permission from the owner.

He lived in a big house, just visible through the trees and though it seemed an imposing place and we guessed the owner was probably someone who cherished his peaceful estate, we still felt quite confident. Several times in the past we had sought a fishing permit in similar situations and we had always succeeded.

Retracing our steps, we came through a hedge onto a lane which we followed until it led us to the gravel drive of the house. Without hesitation, we strode up to the large front porch and rang the bell. There was a stately pause, then a small grey-looking man opened the door.

'Can I help you?' he said in a tone that was slightly too brisk for our liking.

'I hope so,' said Guy.

'We've been looking for a lake to fish,' I said, 'somewhere well off the beaten track.'

'I'm sorry,' said the man, 'but Mr Blakeman does not allow any fishing. Ever.' And he closed the door again.

Sometime later we discovered that the little grey man *was* Mr Blakeman, though naturally it didn't make any difference. He had found his dream and clearly wanted to preserve it. We would have to look elsewhere for ours.

CHAPTER 33

Paradise Found

The time was late May and all the new leaves were as bright as flames. With my two fellow fish-heads, Jasper and Anglepen, I pushed through the dense wood, expecting at any moment to see the blue glimmer of water showing beyond the foliage. Our hand-drawn map showed a large, irregular shaped lake smack in the middle of this great area of wilderness – a wonderful boggy forest of birch, oak and alder. We seemed to have been walking for hours, but there was still no sign of the lake. We weren't particularly worried, though, as we were certain the lake was close. We could smell it – that glorious sweet, almost yeasty smell of an old carp lake. And, besides the familiar scent, we knew it was a carp water because a reliable source had told us so. Not just any old carp water, either. This place had hardly ever been fished and, furthermore, it was alleged to contain monsters.

May was always the month for exploring. It was – and still is – a time when all the best rumours and myths from the previous years were carefully sifted for signs of authenticity. Most of the real humdinger-myths – the ones about record sized carp in overgrown farm ponds – were, of course, sadly fictitious, but there were other stories that had more than a grain of truth. Whenever fishermen gather to talk there will always be a few memorable yarns about secret lakes and lost pools, and a good season will sometimes see a dozen new legends added to my long list. And even if only one of these tales can actually match up to reality then it's always worth a few days in the close season for further enquiry.

We'd heard about this particular lost lake in the summer of '85, when we'd been fishing a river in Sussex. A rather tired looking bream angler (he'd not had a bite all night) told us about a tench water he used to visit, 'a big lily-covered lake, impossible to fish from the banks because of the reeds and silt. But for £2 the old keeper would let you use a boat for the day and – gawd! – what tench! Six and seven pounders sometimes. And once I saw a carp as big as my boat. Hooked one, too; must have been 30lb or more, but, of course, I lost it in the lilies.'

'Is the old keeper still there?' I asked. 'No,' said the bream fisher, 'but he lives in a cottage not far away. He could still tell you a few good stories'.

So we found the old keeper who proved the bream fisher true to his word. We were treated to a marvellous out-

188

pouring of monster stories, though perhaps 'stories' is misleading. 'Epics' would be more accurate. He was a great talker, the keeper, but he ended on a slightly pessimistic note.

Unfortunately, the whole estate had been sold and the keeper didn't hold out much hope that we'd ever be able to fish there.

'But,' he said, 'if you went down to have a look I don't think anyone would complain, especially if you told them I'd sent you.'

We were obviously enthusiastic, but there was still too much fishing to do at our familiar haunts and we didn't have enough time just then to start exploring somewhere new. We would save it for the following May; and now, at last, we were in that merry month.

A few yards to my left, Jasper stopped and pointed. 'There it is,' he said, 'I can see it.' We plunged through a last thicket of oak scrub and came upon a bristling wall of yellow flowering iris. Beyond, lay a wide spread of lily-covered water looking almost exactly as we'd expected – deep, clear, with vast reedbeds forming sheltered bays and lagoons up towards the distant shallows. The air was still and the midday sun quite intense, but there were no signs of basking fish, even though we scanned the surface carefully with binoculars.

We had been walking or rather, squelching, along the marshy shore, hoping to find a break in the reedbeds where we could, at some later, lucky date, perhaps cast a line. We headed up the lake towards the shallows but the reeds just appeared to grow taller and denser.

A hundred yards away we glimpsed a sudden large swirl and were convinced it was caused by a carp. After a minute there was another substantial commotion, right up where the reedbeds appeared to converge. It looked as if a large carp was truffling in the silty, muddy bottom, but there was a deep black, unexpected sidestream that stopped us in our splodgy tracks and it seemed we couldn't get any closer to the disturbance. We pushed back into the wood, following the stream until we came to a place where a dead tree had fallen across it, forming a perfect, if precarious bridge. We walked a tightrope over to the far bank, picked our way round a reed choked quagmire and tried to get back to the lake. But there was no firm ground anywhere and we had to keep going between the trees, where we could at least use the roots as stepping stones while we searched for a proper path.

By the time we had hopped, skipped and jumped back to the water we discovered we'd somehow worked our way right to the end of the main feeder stream, way above the place where we saw the suspected carp. Anglepen had fallen in a ditch, Jasper had filled one boot with black mud and I'd banged my head on a branch as I leapt another sidestream (I almost knocked myself out). We'd come too far, but we couldn't possibly turn back and so we decided to continue until we could cross the feeder stream and come round the lake on the far side.

The stream was easy to cross, for at a high wooden ridge we stumbled upon a weird semi-ornamental grotto, an ancient man-made system of caves where the stream emerged from some subterraneous source. Intrigued, we had to have a brief inspection of this fantastic creation and as we crawled into the darkness we discovered we were wrong about the stream's source. There was no underground spring but something much more interesting. We saw a bright glow ahead of us and, creeping towards it, we realised it was sunlight reflecting from the surface of another lake. We were in a tunnel that was really an overflow channel connecting the lake below with this mysterious lake above (which even the keeper hadn't mentioned).

Emerging into bright sunshine, we staggered to our feet on a grassy dam and gazed, slightly stunned, across the water.

The upper lake was smaller than the lower one, perhaps five acres. It was more sheltered, more intimate and even more seductive, seeming to promise something other than just wondrous carp. Anglepen wandered along to the dam's eastern end and, after a moment, I noticed he was crouching, staring intently into the water. Jasper and I realised instantly what he'd seen and crept quietly up beside him.

'Six of the best!' said Anglepen. There was a weedbed at the corner of the dam and gently drifting around it were six beautiful looking common carp, all over 10 lb with the largest perhaps twice that size. We watched them for a while, whispering our appreciations, then went back across the dam to inspect the other corner, but saw nothing.

Following a firm bankside path along the lake's western side, ducking under willows and alders, we came to an open, treeless area which revealed a sight almost as attractive as the water itself. Bordering the lake was a vast playing field with an old, stately manor house in the distance. We knew it was a playing field and we guessed the great house was now a private school because the grass was swarming with superbly athletic teenage girls, running, jumping and throwing javelins. It must have been sports day.

'Perhaps we could save the carp till later,' suggested Jasper, focusing his binoculars on a particularly long-legged blonde.

'Something must have happened to us in the grotto,' said Anglepen. 'Perhaps this is paradise,' And we all admired the view at maximum magnification, like punters at the Derby.

Because we were staring through our binoculars we didn't see the large Amazonian gym mistress striding purposefully towards us from our left.

'Hey!' she suddenly shouted and we jumped. She was only 10 yards from us and we must have made a deeply suspicious sight: water sodden, mud covered, middle-aged trespassers ogling her innocent girls. What could we say?

We didn't say anything. The situation demanded instant disappearance and within seconds we had vanished back down the overflow tunnel like three rabbits pursued by a bloodthirsty vixen. But we couldn't help laughing.

We trekked round the east side of the lower lake and, though it was still an impressive looking sheet of water, we couldn't appreciate it quite as much as before. It wasn't in the same class as the upper pool.

CHAPTER 34

The Eel Catchers

We didn't want to go to the beach again, so while our parents went there on their own, my brother Nick and I stayed behind at the guest house in Sidmouth, the location for that summer's holiday. It had been perfect seaside weather but, after five scorching days, the beach was losing its appeal. We read our comics, talked about what we'd do when we got back home, then went to look at the river - the Sid - which ran past the house.

It was mostly shallow, clear and fast and although we found a few quieter pools, we couldn't see any fish, not even a minnow. There were lots of ducks, including a Muscovy the like of which we had not encountered before. It was very keen to greet us and probably thought we were in possession of sandwiches. But, as usual, our parents had taken the lunch, made up in a hamper by our kindly landlady, to the beach.

The landlady had a daughter who was, at that moment, sauntering along the bank towards us with her red-headed friend. They asked us if we'd like to go to the cinema with them the following evening and we said 'Only if it's raining' which didn't seem to be the response they were hoping for.

'Why aren't chub in here?' I said after they'd gone. 'It would be a good chub river, but I expect there are only trout.'

We headed upstream, thinking we'd walk to the ford and watch the cars splashing across it. As we came through some trees we spotted three boys our own age wading in the river. One of them was carrying a bucket and the other two were bent forward poking about on the stream bed with what looked like ordinary table forks. They didn't notice us as we approached them and we stopped to watch their slow, intense and mysterious hunting.

Suddenly, one of the boys gave a triumphant yell and held up his fork with a small eel impaled on it. The bucketeer stepped forward, held up his vessel and the eel was plopped inside.

'What are you collecting eels for?' we asked, and the trio jumped and glared at us. We must have looked innocent or harmless enough, because after a moment one of them said, 'Bait.'

'What do you catch on eels?'

'Bass.'

They told us that they didn't actually use them for bait themselves, but a fisherman in the town reckoned that little freshwater eels were superior to sandeels for bass. Furthermore, he gave them a penny per eel.

We offered to help, for nothing, but they reckoned

we'd be more than useless without forks.

'Have you ever tried catching an eel with your bare hands?' asked one of them.

'Yes,' I replied. 'And it is possible.' It was a universal challenge and the five of us enjoyed a wonderfully splashy, finger-stubbing but futile morning. To get at the eels you had to turn over the large stones on the riverbed and if there was one beneath it then you had a split second to press your hand firmly over it before it arrowed itself towards a new hiding place.

Then, while it was pinned down, you had to get the fingers of your free hand round the creature and, keeping your hands together, lift it from the water. Every time, if we managed to get that far, the eel wriggled free again and it was hopeless trying to pursue it until it was under another stone.

By lunchtime we were exhausted and the bucket had no more eels in it. One of the trio suggested that the eel I claimed once to have caught must have been very slow-witted. They took out their forks again - but then the river-keeper appeared, looking serious, and we all ran off through the trees, laughing.

Lunchtime. There were no more excuses. We said goodbye to the eel catchers and headed back to the beach.

CHAPTER 35

Bullheads!

Every child is naturally sceptical about whatever his father likes doing best. But some angling fathers refuse to acknowledge this universal truth and virtually press-gang their sons and daughters into fishing 'because they know they'll love it'. Such behaviour can turn a child off fishing for life.

I've tried to be careful not to force the issue with my own children, to let their own instincts guide them, but knowing all the time that however blasé I am about angling, they cant avoid the subject.

Wherever they go in this house there are bundles of old rods in corners, photographs of fish, reels in various states of disrepair, piles of fishing books, assorted floats on every window sill, hooks in the carpet (amazingly their bare feet have always somehow missed them), smelly nets and creels which often have bluebottles buzzing around in them. Then, whenever we go out we often find time to visit the village pond and feed the carp. And if we visit the river we all end up crawling along bankside weed-beds and peering down at some great pike or chub or trout.

In the summer I occasionally appear at breakfast time, having been out all night, bursting with joy or frustration because of some confrontation with a large fish or sometimes I will just say 'Come and see this!' and they hurry with me to a nearby lake to see the 20lb carp waiting patiently in a sack. I love seeing their faces when they behold a really big fish and yet I realise this could be killing the angler in them. My own angling obsession was sparked off when I was five and saw a carp of about 3lb leaping in a pond. To my inexperienced eyes it looked colossal. And it wasn't until years later that I actually caught my first carp, a tremendous moment in my life, even though the fish weighed a mere 2lb.

Only gradually, slowly, pound by pound, did I work up to fish that really were monstrous. Yet my enjoyment of all those early modest specimens was never diminished by the thought of something more spectacular. I could hardly imagine what a ten-pounder really looked like, let alone anything larger, simply because neither I nor anyone else I knew had ever caught a carp that big.

But nowadays, it seems, everybody has caught a carp that big and my children have all seen enough twenty-pounders to make them appear quite ordinary.

Bullheads!

Sometimes, they all get completely bored by the subject, whether I'm involving them or not. Especially on a wet, cold day in winter, when I come in pale and dripping from the river, but gushing with the joys of barbel fishing, they will look at me with the same contempt they usually reserve for Mr Blobby, Noel Edmonds or John Major.

Months will pass and they – two girls and two boys – will show not the slightest interest in fish or fishing. And then, suddenly, something will happen to spark the old angling gene back into life. For instance, we were all having a summer afternoon tea with a friend who has a little chalk stream forming the boundary of his property. Bernard Venables and his wife Eileen had been invited too, and we were all sitting at a table overlooking the stream, eating strawberries and cream and, of course, talking about fishing.

Even before the strawberries were finished the children were getting restless, but then Alex, who is eight, suddenly became intensely still and boggle-eyed, as if he'd swallowed a wasp. He'd spotted something in the stream and after a brief pause, he shouted 'Bullhead!' and just dropped into the water.

I know, in grown-up terms, dropping into the water to pursue a bullhead with your bare hands is not a true definition of angling, but when you're eight, tickling, snitching and scooping are no less acceptable methods of fishing as fly-casting or long trotting.

201

Within ten minutes Alex had two fine bullheads swimming round and round in a teacup. My other three had also joined him, up to their knees in cold, clear water, carefully feeling under stones for that electrifying little wriggle that only the quickest, nimblest fingers could convert into a small, puffy-faced, beady-eyed fish. And each one was marvelled at in exactly the same way that I might marvel at a big carp,the only difference being that *they* had caught them, they had created them out of nothing, the bullheads were their own miracles.

The transformation had been instant and complete. One moment they were just a bunch of bored, restless kids, the next they were as sharp and alert and quick as four otter cubs.

After an hour or two, Tony, our host, said we should have a look at his pond. It was deep, muddy and weedy, but he promised us it was full of roach.

Inspired by their adventure in the stream my four were quick to gather the travelling kit that always accompanies us in the back of our car. And Bernard, inspired by the sight of the jolly anglers, remembered he too had a rod in the back of his car. Soon there was a wonderful sight as four children – two with rods, one with a net and the youngest (aged three) observing – sat alongside one of England's greatest fishermen, aged 89, all hoping for a roach.

All eyes watched the three quill floats standing in

a line and it was heartening to realise that Bernard was watching with exactly the same intensity and eagerness as the children. Though my tribe probably didn't agree, I felt it was right and proper that the first float to twitch and sink was Bernard's. In came a roach whose brilliant sheen seemed at odds with its murky environment. It was about 8oz and after admiring it, Alex and Camilla quickly re-cast and watched their floats even more intently.

Though Alex is the most active angler of my four children, Camilla, now 11, is always the one who catches the biggest. So it was on this occasion. Her float dipped and when she gently struck her light cane rod went into a shapely curve.

William, aged five, had to wield the landing net, something he always likes to do, even when there's no cause for it. Carefully, Camilla eased a lovely 1lb 4oz redfin into the mesh. She tried to look indifferent as the rest of us congratulated her, but she couldn't help being enchanted by her fish.

Then Alex caught one about three inches long, much to Camilla's gleeful delight. There's nothing like a bit of sibling one-upmanship or, rather, one-upgirlship. It might have caused war or even worse if the afternoon had degenerated into a fishing match, but Bernard was so pleased that everyone had caught a fish, and his humour was so infectious, that they all remained merry and content.

As we drove home that evening I wondered whether their new found enthusiasm would mean I'd have to cancel my next day's carp trip and go roach fishing instead.

'I like roach very much,' said Camilla, who'd never caught one before. 'But I still think I like tench best.'

'Roach are OK,' agreed Alex. 'But they're not as good as eels.'

'I've got tench and eels in my carp lake,' I said with reasonable eagerness. 'Does that mean you're going to want to come fishing with me tomorrow? We may even find some more bullheads.'

'No,' said Camilla. 'I want to record the Top 40.'

'And I want to finish my camp in the woods,' said Alex.

So that was all right then. They've got plenty of time to enjoy their fishing, but life for a child is too diverse to concentrate on fishing alone. And of course this also meant that I could carp fish alone, which I always prefer to do.

But then William perked up. 'I'll come with you, Daddy,' he said. 'Then I can swish your great big carp net about and catch *hundreds* of bullheads!'

CHAPTER 36

The Angler's Lesson

The little suburban council estate could look especially drab at six in the morning, when your body was still complaining about being dragged out of bed so early. My brother Nick, my friend Dave and I would have walked from home weighed down with tackle bags and rod holdalls, trudging up the long boring road that led to the dull huddle of houses.

At a green painted garage door would be waiting half a dozen other anglers who were different from us in that, firstly, they were all grown men, while we were barely into our teens and, secondly, they all looked eager and awake, while we were still half asleep, pale and yawning. They would be cheerful and hearty while we would barely be able to mumble a good morning. I remember the sickly but evocative smells of aftershave, pipe smoke, groundbait and linseed soaked nets, smells that would suddenly intensify after the coach had arrived and we'd all climbed aboard.

And then the world would begin to look a bit better. We and the coachload of other club anglers would speed along deserted Sunday morning roads, away from the towns and the council estates, into a green and pleasant land, heading towards some enchanting sounding place that was still only known to us as a name on the fixture list.

Where was it today? We would turn the name over in our minds and savour a few improbable images. The Thames at Pangbourne, and there we were by the side of a broad, deep river, hauling in colossal bream. The Medway at Oak Lock, and there we were, fishing by an ancient wooden edifice, with the rest of the club cheering us on as we filled our nets with fantastic roach.

I remember vividly an outing we had to the Chichester Canal. It was late August, thirty-two years ago (the roads really were deserted then, early in the morning) and as we headed southwards I asked Fred, the club secretary, what sort of fish we were likely to find.

'Well,' he said, 'there's some good roach, but what we'll all be fishing for are the carp.'

'Carp!' I laughed, and the world, that had been improving anyway, took on a wonderfully golden complexion. All my tiredness left me and even the dreaded thought that the autumn term began next week - a thought that had threatened to overshadow the day - seemed suddenly innocuous. In the hierarchy of magical things, which began with tadpoles and continued upwards through sticklebacks, minnows and gudgeon, the carp was the most magnificent and desirable of them all. No one in our young world had ever caught one before and we counted the few times when we'd actually seen one as sacred days in our calendar. And now we were heading for a water that was, according to Fred, stuffed with them!

After a journey that seemed far to long the coach eventually pulled up right next to the water. We peered eagerly out of the windows, expecting to see the fish leaping up to greet us, but it actually looked rather unexciting - a long, straight, typical canal, with just a few shrubs and willows breaking up the monotony of the banks. But then we noticed dense reed beds and a distant patch of lilies, features that we always associated with carp, and though it was a grey overcast day there was undoubtedly a sort of electricity in the air. We could feel it building up as we gazed at the water and imagined all those great carp lurking, unseen.

As well as the carp, the day was memorable because of the most valuable angling advice I'd ever been given. We were just filing out of the coach when one of the old anglers, a man I'd never spoken to before but who knew of my enthusiasm for carp, caught my sleeve and said,

207

'Before you decide where to fish, wait and see where everyone else goes. When they've all gone, you head off in the opposite direction.' It seemed a sensible idea, but when it came to a decision I guessed that everyone had marched energetically in one direction because that was obviously where all the carp were. And so Nick and Dave and I went that way too, leaving the old fisherman and his friend to shake their heads and walk away towards peace and quiet.

We were to discover the wisdom of his words later on. But for the moment we were just too wild with the thought of golden scales to care about practicalities. We came to a gap in a reedbed that looked sure to hold a few fish and, with maggots and bread as bait, we cast our floats and sat back - or, rather, stood back, because we were too excited to sit, at least for the first hour.

The leaden looking water seemed hardly to stir. The current was imperceptibly slow and our floats rode at anchor with only a couple of shot on the bottom. For an hour we couldn't take our eyes off them, thinking one or other of them was always about to vanish. Nick's was yellow with a red band, Dave's was orange with a black top and mine was red and white. They were all medium sized porcupine quills, but after an hour, as usually happened, we started to lose interest in them. Though we'd rebaited and recast a dozen times not even a pesky roach had come to hold one under. 'I wonder what else is happening?' asked Nick and we went off down the towpath to find out.

'Where are all these carp?' we asked Fred, who, likewise, hadn't had a bite yet.

'Give them time.' he said. 'The morning's not even half over yet and we're not packing up till five o'clock. Have patience.'

But fisherboys never have patience. Even in the presence of the carp gods it was impossible to sit still for long, especially when no one else was catching anything. However, as we were walking back to our rods (and being told off by one of the other members for talking too loudly) something sensational happened. A man on the opposite bank hooked a fish that we soon realised must be a carp. And not only that, it was a big one. He'd been fishing a float just a yard from the trailing branches of a big overhanging willow. We'd noticed the spot when we first passed by and agreed that it was a place we would have chosen. Now here was a proper carp angler with his rod in a proper bend, unlike any bend we'd seen in our rods (except when we hooked the bottom). He played the fish superbly, managing to turn its head from the sunken branches and keep it circling in clear water in front of him.

We watched, awe-struck, as it finally came towards the net, wallowing amazingly on the surface so that we could see the bright gold of the flanks. Then out it came and, even though he was only fifteen yards away, the angler and his fish disappeared behind a wall of bankside reeds for the unhooking ceremony.

'How big is it?' we shouted across. There was an answering mutter which we didn't quite catch but which sounded like 'twenty pounds'. So twenty pounds it was. And of course that was just the sort of weight we'd had in mind for now we could tell all our friends that we'd actually seen a mythical twenty-pounder. We stood, silently, like a church congregation waiting for a final blessing. And then the angler reappeared and we all saw the great fish again, being gently returned to the canal.

'Oh yes,' we said in hushed whisper. 'Definitely twenty pounds.' Even though it was probably only about five – or less.

Our enthusiasm restored, we hurried back to our rods for another intense bout of fishing. And we didn't have to wait long. After about ten minutes, Dave's float slid under. One moment there were three floats and the next there were only two.

Dave struck and an incredible golden scaled fish came up through the surface and hung for a miraculous second in the air. Then it crashed back, ploughed off across the canal, broke Dave's line and everyone began shouting and dancing around. We had only just calmed down when it was time to pack up. No one had had another bite. But it didn't matter; Dave had made contact with one of those phenomenal creatures, a fish that might have weighed about three pounds and which would haunt our dreams for several nights to follow. We had achieved half a miracle, which was, to be honest, more than we'd expected.

But when we went to watch the weighing in, and after a roach or two had been recorded, the antisocial old chap who'd offered his advice unparcelled a giant keepnet and revealed something more than a miracle. We stood dumb-struck as he weighed in at least a dozen fabulous carp. Was this a dream or a nightmare? We hadn't imagined such a sight possible and yet we knew we'd always regret seeing it because if we'd followed the advice then we, too, might have shared that canal shattering catch. Certainly, the angler's solitary friend had also managed four or five terrific fish (all taken on "stewed wheat"), and even if we had not caught anything ourselves, we could, if we'd been there, at least have witnessed the true (golden) scale of the achievement.

Fred shook the angler's hand and announced him the clear winner of the club sweepstake. Of course we didn't give a maggot for sweepstakes or any other kind of official competition. We didn't care whether anyone knew what we'd caught or not. All we really cared about was the carp – and we had just missed an unrepeatable opportunity for our first one. There would be no more trips to the Chichester Canal that season, and Nick, Dave and I never went back. I didn't say a word, and after he'd released his fish, the old boy just smiled at me. I smiled too, sheepishly, and he obviously knew I'd learnt my lesson, the only one I shall always remember.